W9-BYD-745

NAT
TURNER

NAT TURNER

Terry Bisson

Senior Consulting Editor
Nathan Irvin Huggins
Director
W.E.B. Du Bois Institute for Afro-American Research
Harvard University

CHELSEA HOUSE PUBLISHERS
New York   Philadelphia

Chelsea House Publishers

Editor-in-Chief   Nancy Toff
Executive Editor   Remmel T. Nunn
Managing Editor   Karyn Gullen Browne
Copy Chief   Juliann Barbato
Picture Editor   Adrian G. Allen
Art Director   Giannella Garrett
Manufacturing Manager   Gerald Levine

Black Americans of Achievement

Senior Editor   Richard Rennert

Staff for NAT TURNER

Associate Editor   Perry King
Assistant Editor   Gillian Bucky
Copy Editor   Karen Hammonds
Deputy Copy Chief   Ellen Scordato
Editorial Assistant   Susan DeRosa
Associate Picture Editor   Juliette Dickstein
Picture Researcher   Toby Greenberg
Senior Designer   Laurie Jewell
Design Assistant   Laura Lang
Production Coordinator   Joseph Romano
Cover Illustration   Alan J. Nahigian

3   5   7   9   8   6   4   2

Library of Congress Cataloging in Publication Data
Bisson, Terry.
  Nat Turner.

  (Black Americans of Achievement)
  Includes index.
  Summary: A biography of the slave and preacher who, be-
lieving that God wanted him to free the slaves, led a major
revolt in 1831.
  1. Turner, Nat, 1800?–1831—Juvenile literature.
2. Slaves—Virginia—Biography—Juvenile literature.
3. Southampton Insurrection, 1831—Juvenile literature.
[1. Turner, Nat, 1800?–1831.   2. Slaves.
3. Afro-Americans—Biography]   I. Title.   II. Series.
F232.S7T873   1988   975.5'5503'0924 [B] [92]
87-37559
ISBN 1-55546-613-3

    0-7910-0214-4   (pbk.)

CONTENTS

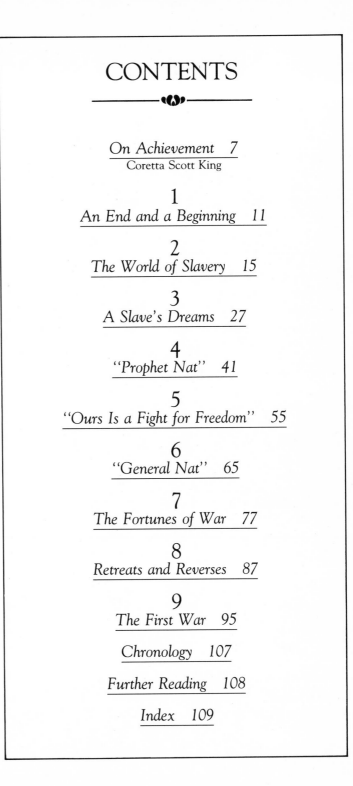

BLACK
AMERICANS
OF
ACHIEVEMENT

MUHAMMAD ALI
heavyweight champion

RICHARD ALLEN
*founder of the
African Methodist
Episcopal church*

LOUIS ARMSTRONG
musician

JAMES BALDWIN
author

BENJAMIN BANNEKER
*scientist and
mathematician*

MARY MCLEOD BETHUNE
educator

BLANCHE K. BRUCE
politician

RALPH BUNCHE
diplomat

GEORGE WASHINGTON CARVER
botanist

CHARLES WADDELL CHESTNUTT
author

PAUL CUFFE
abolitionist

FREDERICK DOUGLASS
abolitionist editor

CHARLES R. DREW
physician

W. E. B. DUBOIS
educator and author

PAUL LAURENCE DUNBAR
poet

DUKE ELLINGTON
bandleader and composer

RALPH ELLISON
author

ELLA FITZGERALD
singer

MARCUS GARVEY
black-nationalist leader

PRINCE HALL
social reformer

WILLIAM H. HASTIE
educator and politician

MATTHEW A. HENSON
explorer

CHESTER HIMES
author

BILLIE HOLIDAY
singer

JOHN HOPE
educator

LENA HORNE
entertainer

LANGSTON HUGHES
poet

JAMES WELDON JOHNSON
author

SCOTT JOPLIN
composer

MARTIN LUTHER KING, JR.
civil rights leader

JOE LOUIS
heavyweight champion

MALCOLM X
militant black leader

THURGOOD MARSHALL
Supreme Court justice

ELIJAH MUHAMMAD
religious leader

JESSE OWENS
champion athlete

GORDON PARKS
photographer

SIDNEY POITIER
actor

ADAM CLAYTON POWELL, JR.
political leader

A. PHILIP RANDOLPH
labor leader

PAUL ROBESON
singer and actor

JACKIE ROBINSON
baseball great

JOHN RUSSWURM
publisher

SOJOURNER TRUTH
antislavery activist

HARRIET TUBMAN
antislavery activist

NAT TURNER
slave revolt leader

DENMARK VESEY
slave revolt leader

MADAME C. J. WALKER
entrepreneur

BOOKER T. WASHINGTON
educator

WALTER WHITE
political activist

RICHARD WRIGHT
author

ON
ACHIEVEMENT

Coretta Scott King

BEFORE YOU BEGIN this book, I hope you will ask yourself what the word excellence means to you. I think that it's a question we should all ask, and keep asking as we grow older and change. Because the truest answer to it should never change. When you think of excellence, perhaps you think of success at work; or of becoming wealthy; or meeting the right person, getting married, and having a good family life.

Those important goals are worth striving for, but there is a better way to look at excellence. As Martin Luther King, Jr., said in one of his last sermons, "I want you to be first in love. I want you to be first in moral excellence. I want you to be first in generosity. If you want to be important, wonderful. If you want to be great, wonderful. But recognize that he who is greatest among you shall be your servant."

My husband, Martin Luther King, Jr., knew that the true meaning of achievement is service. When I met him, in 1952, he was already ordained as a Baptist preacher and was working towards a doctoral degree at Boston University. I was studying at the New England Conservatory and dreamed of accomplishments in music. We married a year later, and after I graduated the following year we moved to Montgomery, Alabama. We didn't know it then, but our notions of achievement were about to undergo a dramatic change.

You may have read or heard about what happened next. What began with the boycott of a local bus line grew into a national movement, and by the time he was assassinated in 1968 my husband had fashioned a black movement powerful enough to shatter forever the practice of racial segregation. What you may not have read about is where he got his method for resisting injustice without compromising his religious beliefs.

He got the strategy of nonviolence from a man of a different race, who lived in a distant country, and even practiced a different religion. The man was Mahatma Gandhi, the great leader of India, who devoted his life to serving humanity in the spirit of love and nonviolence. It was in these principles that Martin discovered his method for social reform. More than anything else, those two principles were the key to his achievements.

This book is about black Americans who served society through the excellence of their achievements. It forms a part of the rich history of black men and women in America—a history of stunning accomplishments in every field of human endeavor, from literature and art to science, industry, education, diplomacy, athletics, jurisprudence, even polar exploration.

Not all of the people in this history had the same ideals, but I think you will find something that all of them have in common. Like Martin Luther King, Jr., they all decided to become "drum majors" and serve humanity. In that principle—whether it was expressed in books, inventions, or song—they found something outside themselves to use as a goal and a guide. Something that showed them a way to serve others, instead of living only for themselves.

Reading the stories of these courageous men and women not only helps us discover the principles that we will use to guide our own lives, but it teaches us about our black heritage and about America itself. It is crucial for us to know the heroes and heroines of our history and to realize that the price we paid in our struggle for equality in America was dear. But we must also understand that we have gotten as far as we have partly because America's democratic system and ideals made it possible.

We still are struggling with racism and prejudice. But the great men and women in this series are a tribute to the spirit of our democratic ideals and the system in which they have flourished. And that makes their stories special, and worth knowing. ◄○►

NAT
TURNER

1

AN END
AND
A BEGINNING

———— ❧ ————

I T WAS A perfect day for a hanging.

The autumn air was brisk as an eager crowd gathered at the edge of town. A hanging—especially the hanging of a slave—was a popular public spectacle in pre–Civil War Virginia, almost as exciting as a horse race. Fried chicken and biscuits were unpacked. Men took long pulls at the apple brandy that was Southampton County's most famous product. Older children ripped through the gathering crowd, while the little ones tugged at their mothers' skirts, wondering what all the excitement was about.

Suddenly, a mother stood and hoisted her baby to her shoulder. A father pulled his son from play and commanded him to pay attention. A wagon was approaching from the center of town, with armed men on horses riding in front and behind.

Nat Turner—a compact, muscular man about 30 years old—rode in the wagon, bound in chains. His broad, handsome African features were calm and composed; his brown eyes scanned the crowd without wavering. If he was looking for a friendly face, he was disappointed. All of the faces that he saw were white, and most were twisted with hatred. A few weeks before, when he was captured, the crowd had taunted him and spat at him, then beaten him with ropes and sticks. But on this day they were silent.

Turner's band of slave revolutionaries carved a trail of death in Virginia during their fierce bid for freedom in 1831. Turner met his own death with courage and dignity on the Southampton County "hanging tree," shown here as it appeared 60 years later.

Turner was imprisoned in the Southampton County Jail (shown here) after his capture. Calling himself a martyr for the cause of black freedom, the condemned man asked his accusers, "Was not Christ crucified?"

The wagon stopped. The jailer helped the prisoner down, then whispered in his ear as he led him toward the twisted old oak that served Southampton County as a hanging tree. The jailer had asked him if he had any last words that he wanted to say.

Turner shook his head. He had already had his say. In a long interview conducted in jail a few days before, he had told the story of the slave rebellion that he had led. That would be his statement for the world. "I am ready" was all he would now say.

Without flinching, Turner allowed a thick hemp rope to be put over his neck and the knot pulled snug. Ignoring the breathless crowd, he looked up for one last time at the autumn sky, towering with clouds. Then, without a flicker, he closed his great, dark eyes on the world.

The other end of the rope was thrown over a high limb. A ripple of excitement ran through the crowd as a few white men especially chosen for this honor spat on their hands and took hold of the rope. As they yanked the doomed man off his feet, the crowd gasped in anticipation.

Yet they were denied the spectacle that they had come to see. Turner died as he had lived: with the dignity and courage of a leader of men, and with a measure of mystery as well. Hoisted toward the Heaven that he firmly believed was preparing to receive him with honors, he hung perfectly still, as if already dead; he hung without a kick or a twitch, determined even in his last moments to deny his enemies the satisfaction of watching his torment.

It was Turner's last act, and it spooked the crowd. "Not a limb or a muscle was observed to move," an awed eyewitness reported.

Unnerved, disappointed, uneasy, the white people of southeastern Virginia went home—some to pitiful hardscrabble farms, some to vast plantations. Later in the evening, as their slaves watered and bedded the horses, they said their prayers, lit their lamps, and kissed their children good night, as they usually did.

But this night was also different. This night they locked their doors. They checked the pistols under their beds; they primed the shotguns leaning against the bedroom walls. They woke up at every moaning of the wind, every cracking branch, every cooing dove.

For Turner and the men who rode with him had put an end to the peaceful sleep of Virginia. By attacking slavery with the sword, they had shattered the complacency of the South. By organizing and leading the most successful slave revolt in American history, Turner had drowned in blood the absurd lie that blacks were happy as slaves and would submit forever to be the beasts of burden of whites.

Now everyone—both blacks and whites—knew that slavery would be stopped. It was only a matter of time. ❧

A preacher and mystic, Turner claimed that he had been chosen by God to bring about an end to the slave system. Although Turner was captured and hanged after his revolt, his bold act of defiance against the tyranny of slavery proved to be an inspiring symbol to other black rebels.

2

THE WORLD
OF
SLAVERY

N AT TURNER WAS born in Southampton County, Virginia, in 1800. According to legend, his mother was so determined not to subject him to a life of slavery that she tried to kill him as soon as he was born. She was tied to her bed and held away from him until she calmed down.

After that brief moment, however, Nat's mother lavished love and affection on him. To make him grow proud and independent, she continually told him of the greatness of his African heritage—even before he was old enough to understand her. If she could not keep him from being born into slavery, at least she could keep his young mind from being enslaved.

While Nat was still very young, his parents and grandmother searched his head and body for bumps and marks that were, in African religion and folklore, signs of prophecy. They then told him—and any others who would listen—that he was destined for great things. In his *Confessions*, written after the 1831 rebellion, Nat emphasized his parents' strong influence on his life by saying, "My father and mother strengthened me in this, my first impressions: that I was to be a Prophet."

While Nat was growing up in Virginia, he was surrounded by what was one of the cruelest systems of slavery ever established by mankind. The slave

Slave caravans transported yoked and bound captives from Africa's inland villages to ports on the coast. Turner's mother was among the tens of millions of Africans who were loaded onto ships and carried off to the Americas.

system in 19th-century America was built from an international slave-trade network that was founded in the 1520s. Men and women were stolen from their homes and farms in Africa, brought by Europeans to the colonies in the Americas, and condemned to perpetual servitude. For most, there was no hope, no reprieve from life as a slave.

The activities of this international slave-trade network remained legal until 1808, when the importation of slaves was outlawed by the governments of Great Britain and the United States. But because the legislation that abolished the importation of slaves was not widely enforced, slaves were still being imported from Africa while Nat was growing up in the early 1800s.

American slaveowners treated African-born slaves much more ruthlessly than they treated other people who worked as servants and laborers. Indentured servants who came to America from Europe worked for

An escaped slave named Margaret Garner stabbed to death two of her children to prevent them from being recaptured by slave-catchers. According to some accounts, Turner's mother similarly tried to kill him so that he would be spared from a life in slavery.

an agreed-upon period of time—five years, seven years—after which they were free. However, captured Africans remained as slaves until the day they died, and their children were regarded as slaves from the moment they were born. Even those few blacks who managed to buy their freedom or were released from slavery had no real freedom—neither in the British colonies nor after the colonies became the United States.

In the North as well as in the South, free blacks were denied almost all legal rights, including the right to vote, to live where they wanted, and to defend themselves or their property in court. Even when free blacks managed to scrape together a little land or some tools, or build or buy a house, their property might be taken away from them by whites. This was done through legal trickery or outright violence, in the same way that these blacks or their ancestors had been stolen from their homeland. Free blacks were sometimes even kidnapped and sold back into slavery.

In America, the slave system was based on a doctrine—still prevalent in parts of the world today—called white supremacy. The followers of this doctrine considered whites to be "more human" than other people. Consequently, whites had more rights to property, liberty, and happiness than any other people in the world. This doctrine conveniently allowed whites to enslave Africans and steal the land of the indigenous American people (whom the European settlers had mistakenly called Indians) with a clear—or almost clear—conscience.

Prejudice is as old as humanity itself and has been practiced by all peoples. However, white supremacy—holding that entire races are actually subhuman (somewhere between beasts and men)—was originally formulated in Europe, and it led to the cruelty of American slavery. The political and economic ef-

$1200 TO 1250 DOLLARS! FOR NEGROES!!

THE undersigned wishes to purchase a large lot of NEGROES for the New Orleans market. I will pay $1200 to $1250 for No. 1 young men, and $850 to $1000 for No. 1 young women. In fact I will pay more for likely

NEGROES,

Than any other trader in Kentucky. My office is adjoining the Broadway Hotel, on Broadway, Lexington, Ky., where I or my Agent can always be found.

WM. F. TALBOTT.

LEXINGTON, JULY 2, 1853.

The slave trade was a profitable business for both northern shipping merchants and southern plantation owners. Strong, able-bodied field hands commanded huge prices, especially in the Deep South.

fects of this doctrine are still seen today in the depressed conditions under which blacks live in many parts of the world. The psychological effects are difficult to see and are even harder for whites to imagine. As David Walker, a free black abolitionist, wrote in his passionate *Appeal* of 1829:

> I call upon the professing Christians, I call upon the philanthropist, I call upon the very tyrant himself, to show me a page of history . . . which maintains that the Egyptians heaped the insupportable insult upon the children of Israel, by telling them they were not of the human family. Can the whites deny this charge? [Has not] Mr. [Thomas] Jefferson declared to the world, that we are inferior, both in the endowments of our bodies and our minds?

Composer of the Declaration of Independence, Thomas Jefferson supported the gradual abolition of slavery in the United States. Nonetheless, he owned many slaves and believed that blacks were inferior to whites. This page from his accounts book lists the slaves who worked at his Monticello estate.

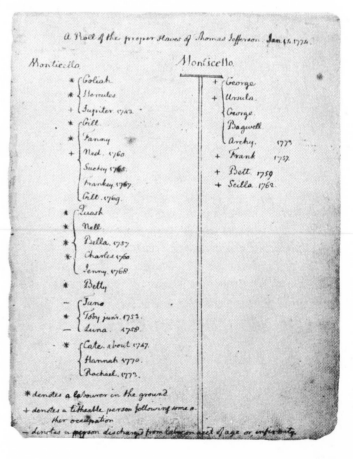

For more than 200 years—from the early 1600s until the 1860s—slaves in America produced rice, sugar, indigo, cotton, tobacco, coal, gold, lumber, and hemp worth billions of dollars. They cleared and fenced the land, built the barns and houses, plowed, harvested, and produced the wealth on which the growth of the United States was based. Yet neither they nor their descendants have ever been paid for this labor or compensated for the crime of being kidnapped from their native land.

This was the form of slavery that was practiced in the United States until it was abolished in 1865, after the Civil War, and it may have been even harsher than the form of slavery that was employed by either the ancient Egyptians or the ancient Romans. The

Slavery was a common practice in the Roman Empire and other civilizations of the ancient world. Wealthy people considered it a mark of distinction to own many house servants.

Slave traders rarely showed any sympathy for their captives when they were auctioned off and their family ties were severed. Slaves were considered easier to train once they were completely cut off from their friends and relatives.

master of an American or Caribbean slave was usually a middle-class farmer who lived on credit, was always in debt, and had to push his slaves to produce more every year. Therefore, the slave's true master was the worldwide commodity system and its bottomless hunger for cotton and sugar.

Slaves in the South worked six or six and a half days a week, from sunup to sundown (from "can see" to "can't see"). The average slaveowner spent an estimated seven dollars a year per slave for food and about the same amount for clothing. Even at a time when seven dollars might equal a month's wages for a white farmworker, this amount was low enough to make slavery an extremely attractive system for slaveowners.

Historians sometimes write about how American slaves were rarely mistreated, how slaveowners were often kind, and how even those who were not kind were hardly stupid enough to mistreat their own valuable property any more than they would mistreat a horse or a piano. Yet people often mistreat animals, either through ignorance or malice. And while it is true that people rarely mistreat an object as valuable as a piano, a piano rarely rebels or resists.

Slaves often did resist, in big ways and small. They refused to work, or they worked slowly or "stupidly," sabotaging tools or crops. They ran away, joining the Indians or forming societies of their own, which were called Maroon societies, deep in the hills or the swamps. Traces of these societies exist today in Haiti, Guyana, and Jamaica. Their legacy can also be seen in the African coloring of the Florida Seminoles, who were a civilized people and took in runaways from the barbarism of slavery. There were even remnants of a Maroon society, Coe Ridge, in the hills of Kentucky until the 1940s.

However, most slaves—like most people—were not brave enough or lucky enough to run away and start a new life in the wilderness. For them, escape took the form of religion and storytelling—dreaming of another, better world—or else they put their hopes in their children, as so many people of all races do, even today.

It was into this strange, cruel world that an African teenager—said by legend to be a queen of the Sudan—was kidnapped in 1793. (Many of the stories that have been told about this young woman, who became Nat's mother, are really legends. Although not all legends are based on fact, they are still important because they tell us much about the hopes and dreams of the people who relate them.) Legend says that she was a queen, and perhaps she was: When wars took place between rival African states, many royal Africans were captured by their enemies and sold to European slave traders.

The young woman's owner called her Nancy, but this was not her real name (just as Nat was probably not the name that she gave to her son after he was born). Her real name was stolen from her—along with her language, her homeland, and her customs—because the slave system in America was threatened by slaves who remained bound to their original culture. Being given Christian names helped to complete their sense of alienation from their homeland and destroy their former identity.

It is said that Nat's mother was kidnapped from the ancient lands of the upper Nile and marched a thousand miles to the sea, chained in a long caravan with other captives, and then locked in the hold of a ship. There began the dreaded Middle Passage, a genocidal nightmare that rivals in horror the Holocaust that was carried out by Nazi Germany in the 1930s and the 1940s. As many as 5 to 10 million Africans died on the journey across the Atlantic Ocean, crammed into the airless holds of specially designed ships, where they could neither move nor sit nor stand. Only 18 inches of space were allotted for each man, woman, and child.

Once a day (when the weather permitted it), the slaves were taken on deck from the airless dungeon of the hold and were slopped like hogs with cornmeal from a barrel, splashed down with salt water, and then forced with whips back down into the darkness and their chains. Those who could make it to the side of the ship sometimes hurled themselves or their children over the side and into the ocean. Dead and sickly slaves were also thrown overboard by the crew. It is said that the shark population grew a thousand-fold during slavery and that they followed the ships in great gray schools under water. Folklore even says that it was the slave trade that introduced sharks to human flesh and made them man-eaters.

Those Africans who survived the Middle Passage were unloaded into dockside slave pens in Jamaica, Barbados, Georgia, and Virginia. They were cleaned up and fattened for a few weeks like cattle (and often branded with red-hot irons as well), then stripped naked, inspected from tooth to toe, and sold at auction. Babies were sold from their mothers' arms.

The cargo holds on slave ships were hellish prisons in which chained captives were kept penned close together and were given little food or water. Many slaves died or committed suicide during the torturous voyage across the Atlantic Ocean.

The African teenager who was to become Nat's mother arrived in Norfolk, Virginia, in 1797. She was angry, rebellious, and (although she probably tried not to show it) heartbroken because she was never to see her parents or loved ones again, never to see her home once more. If the legend is true and she was from the upper Nile, then she grew up in a land of ancient cities, awesome temples, and centers of learning and trade. What, then, did she think when she saw the slave ports of Tidewater Virginia, the crude cabins and log huts, the hogs running in the streets?

She was bought by a farmer named Benjamin Turner in 1799 and taken to his home in Southampton County. As crude as Norfolk was, one can only imagine what this teenager from the cradle of civilization thought of this region's scrub pine and swamp wilderness, where even the wealthiest planter lived in a board shack or a two-story "dogtrot" cabin. Southampton County in 1800 was a backwater. It took two days through the Great Dismal Swamp to get there from Norfolk; two days through the pine forests to get there from Richmond, the capital of Virginia; and a day to get there from the more settled areas of North Carolina, which were just to the south.

Benjamin Turner christened his newly acquired human property "Nancy," and her real name was lost to history. It is not known what her language was; it is said that she resisted speaking English for many years. Because she was rebellious, she was beaten often and severely.

At Benjamin Turner's farm, Nancy met "Old Bridget," who would soon become her mother-in-law. Although Bridget was only a generation away from Africa herself, it is doubtful that the two women spoke the same language; Africa, like Europe, is a continent of many tongues, and slaveowners were careful to separate slaves who spoke the same lan-

The agents of wealthy southern planters regularly attended slave auctions in search of promising workers. Occasional rebellions in the auction houses' slave pens were suppressed by the local militia.

The successful revolt against French rule carried out in the 1790s by slaves in Haiti was a tremendous inspiration to American slaves. Toussaint L'Ouverture (shown here) led the rebellion that gave birth to the first black nation in the Western hemisphere.

guage. Perhaps, in a final irony, the African teenager had to learn English so that she could converse with other Africans.

In her loneliness and desolation, Nancy was given—willingly or not, we will never know—to Bridget's son. Before the year 1799 was out, she was pregnant with a child who would become the property of Benjamin Turner, Esq., of Southampton County, Virginia.

Although the name of Nat's father has not been recorded, we know that he was only two generations removed from Africa himself, and we know from his later actions that he possessed a proud, rebellious spirit. We can only imagine that he loved his son and, like Nat's mother and grandmother, raised him with the belief that he was destined to be more than just a Virginia farmer's chattel.

Many changes and portents coincided with the start of the 19th century. To the south, on the French-ruled island of Santo Domingo, a fierce slave revolt was blazing into success. Haiti, the first black republic, was being wrested from the control of the French planters by the great black general Toussaint L'Ouverture. Slaveowners from Brazil to Virginia trembled in their boots at Toussaint's success. Slaves were rising up, arming themselves, killing their white oppressors, seizing the land, and setting up their own government. Is it any wonder that Thomas Jefferson and the Founding Fathers feared that their own slaves might do the same?

New laws were passed restricting free blacks. Garrisons were built and guns were stockpiled in every town, until every 10th person in Virginia was part of the armed militia. Slaves were forbidden to read or write, and on Sundays they were taught that slavery was blessed by God and sanctified in the Bible. Still, the slaves plotted rebellion. In southern Virginia, a group of slaves rose up and killed their overseers. They were hanged.

The offices of slave dealers were common sights on the streets of southern cities. Many stores that sold farm equipment and livestock also held slave auctions.

Then, in Richmond, also at the turn of the century, a slave named Gabriel Prosser organized the biggest slave revolt ever planned until then. Prosser even had a new flag made, saying that the Africans were going to take what the whites had taken from the British only a few years before: independence. Prosser's rebels intended to spare those few whites who had shown sympathy for the Africans and opposition to the slave system—mostly Quakers and some Methodists.

However, Prosser's rebellion was discovered. The leaders were captured, and the Americans showed their love of liberty by hanging all those Africans who had conspired to gain it.

During that same year, 500 miles to the north, John Brown was born—a white man who would go down in history as an enemy of slavery and a friend to the Africans.

It was in this portentous year of 1800 that Nat Turner was born. 🌿

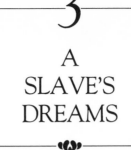

3

A
SLAVE'S
DREAMS

WHAT WAS LIFE like for a slave child in the early 1800s? For years, the old folks remembered slavery days as "frock time" because women and children—boys as well as girls—went around in shapeless, baglike dresses or frocks. Nat did, too, until he was 12 years old.

Home for a typical slave family was a 16-foot square, windowless log hut with a dirt floor. Bed was a cornshuck-stuffed pallet in the corner or, for the fortunate child, perhaps a little loft. Breakfast was hoecakes (fried cornbread). Dinner was more cornbread, cabbage, black-eyed peas, and molasses. On Sundays or holidays there might be a little pigsfeet or fatback—leftovers from the whites at the "home house." Perhaps the head of the family had sneaked away during the week and snared a possum or caught some lazy catfish in one of the swampy ponds around Southampton County. As related in the "Uncle Remus" fables published by Joel Chandler Harris in the late 1800s, the slaves were clever at getting by and at coming up with little extra treats for their children.

A slave child was expected to start earning his or her keep at an early age. (This was true in industrial

Cotton was the chief crop grown on the farms in Virginia, where Turner was raised. Because the plant quickly exhausted the soil, the center of cotton production gradually moved to more recently settled areas in the Deep South and the West.

27

At an early age, slave children were put to work shelling peas and doing other light chores.

England, too, where free white children—at least, those of the poor—who were as young as eight were put to work in the mills and mines.) In Virginia, slave children were put to work around the yard and kitchen from about the age of 7 and were sent to the fields at the age of 12. Their childhood was brief.

Still, slave children managed to have some fun—at least when the white slaveowners were off to one of their many prayer meetings. Then there were children all over the place, bubbling over with joy and mischief. There was play—sometimes even with white children who were too young to understand that someday their playmates would be their property. It is said that one of the few whites who was spared by Nat's army during its bloody march across Southampton County was a man with whom Nat had played while he was a boy.

As in many agricultural or peasant societies where the women work in the fields with the men, the very young were watched over by the very old. Nat, like so many black children, grew up at the knees of the old folks—the ones with the stories, myths, and legends of their beloved African homeland still in their hearts. His early days were filled with stories about his heritage told to him not only by his mother but by others as well.

Nat's grandmother, Bridget, who had become a Christian, taught him about Christianity and probably showed him how to read as well. Nat was able to read at an early age, perhaps as young as five. This was very unusual in a country where most of the adult whites were illiterate.

There are several legends that are told about how Nat learned to read. He himself said that the alphabet "came to him" in a vision, the letters burning themselves into fallen leaves on the ground. He may have sincerely believed in such miracles, or he may have just been keeping a secret—that the old slaves taught the young ones some forbidden things.

Some historians maintain that Benjamin Turner's family taught Nat how to read. However, it was a criminal offense to teach a slave to read in those days, and although Benjamin Turner was a liberal Methodist, it is not likely that he was so liberal that he would attempt such a thing. Yet he did allow Nat to read once he discovered that Nat knew how; he even encouraged it—as long as Nat's reading was confined to the Bible.

Nat was also instructed in religion by his grandmother. He became a Christian, although it appears that he took less to the New Testament and its lessons of forgiveness, about which the slaveowners were always preaching to the slaves, and more to the stern righteousness, blood, and thunder of the Old Tes-

Although masters were forbidden from teaching their slaves how to read, some slaveowners organized Sunday school lessons. Turner was one of the few slaves who learned how to read, and he spent much time studying the words of the Old Testament's prophets and warriors.

tament prophets. Once he became a Christian, religion and freedom became tied together in his mind.

It is probable that Nat learned to respect African religion as well. One of the most trusted leaders of his rebellion was a "conjure man" trained in African folklore, medicines, rituals, and charms. From these religious teachings, Nat learned to be responsible and respectful to his elders.

Nat's father ran away from the Turner farm when Nat was only eight or nine. This must have been both the saddest and the happiest day of his young life: to know that your parent is gone, yet to know that he has flown to freedom. What a conflict of feeling the news of his father's escape must have produced in the young boy's heart! Although he missed his father, the example of his courage and daring was to stay with Nat all of his life.

One story has it that Nat's father escaped to the North; another has it that he made it back to Africa, to Liberia. However, another and more chilling story is still told around Southampton County. It says that Nat's father was betrayed after his escape and was sold to the turpentine plantations in Georgia, which few men survived. The story also says that when Nat later discovered that his father was not free but was

According to some historians, the farmhouse shown here belonged to Turner's first master, Benjamin Turner.

probably dead, it was the bitterest disappointment of his life.

Nat began to work all of the time when he was 12 years old, and the full bitterness of slavery was soon upon him. He worked from dawn to dusk plowing, hoeing, weeding, building fences, feeding animals, and gathering in crops. His owners were not rich, nor were they idle; they were farmers who sometimes even worked in the fields alongside their slaves. But as hard as the Turners worked, they were getting something in return for their efforts. They owned the land, and they owned the crops; the improvements as well as the profits were theirs.

As Nat toiled day and night for nothing, he watched as his own family—and his own people—sank deeper and deeper into ignorance and slavery. Because he knew how to read and knew about his heritage, he was better off than most other slaves. How many slaves knew nothing else but slavery? How many generations would it be before his people lost all memory of their former greatness, including their languages, their religions, and their history? How many gener-

While growing up, Turner sat by the fireplace in his cabin and listened to his grandmother and the other black elders tell stories about Africa, Jesus and his disciples, and slaves who escaped to freedom.

ations before all of their heroes were replaced by American heroes who were white? Before long, the slaves would become what their owners wanted them to be: not men but beasts of burden.

As Nat worked the sandy fields behind a plow, he thought deeply on these matters. One day, he claimed to have heard a voice that told him to seek "the Kingdom of Heaven." Perhaps this voice was as real to him as the voices in biblical times were to the prophets in the Old Testament; perhaps this voice was part of a religious parable made up by Nat so that white Christians would recognize that he was a human being just like themselves. In either case, the Kingdom of Heaven meant only one thing to a slave: freedom. However, Nat did not know at this point if the voice meant freedom just for himself, for his family and friends, or for his entire people.

When Nat was 20 years old, Virginia fell into an economic depression that lowered the price of land, farm commodities, and slaves. The price of cotton soon dropped dramatically, from 30 cents a pound to 10 cents a pound. The other main cash crops in Southampton County—apples, which were made into a crude brandy that was the most famous local specialty, and peanuts—also fell drastically in price.

Many of the farmers started to sell their land and move west and south, to Kentucky, Tennessee, Alabama, and Mississippi. Those farmers who managed to hold on to their land sometimes saw their children leave. Few new settlers moved in. The opening of the American frontier further helped to depopulate the Tidewater area—especially Southampton County, with its sandy, worn-out soil.

Because of the depression, slavery did not prove to be as profitable as it had once been in the part of Virginia where Nat lived. Many slaves were sold and transported out west and down south. Some bought their freedom with the money that they had managed

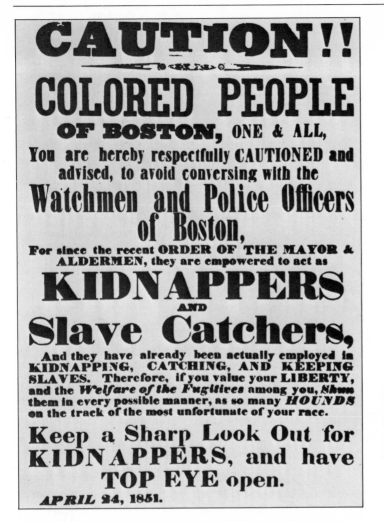

CAUTION!!

COLORED PEOPLE

OF BOSTON, ONE & ALL,

You are hereby respectfully CAUTIONED and advised, to avoid conversing with the

Watchmen and Police Officers of Boston,

For since the recent ORDER OF THE MAYOR & ALDERMEN, they are empowered to act as

KIDNAPPERS

AND

Slave Catchers,

And they have already been actually employed in KIDNAPPING, CATCHING, AND KEEPING SLAVES. Therefore, if you value your LIBERTY, and the *Welfare of the Fugitives* among you, *Shun* them in every possible manner, as so many *HOUNDS* on the track of the most unfortunate of your race.

Keep a Sharp Look Out for KIDNAPPERS, and have TOP EYE open.

APRIL 24, 1851.

Pushed beyond his limit by a harsh slave overseer, Turner became a fugitive for 30 days before he decided to return to his master. Even if Turner had escaped to the North, he still would have faced the danger of being kidnapped by slavecatchers who roamed the streets of cities such as Boston.

to scrape together; not only could most slaveowners use the money, but when it came time for them to buy a new slave, one would not cost very much. Still other slaves were given their freedom. There was even talk of legally abolishing slavery.

In the early 1820s, there were about 1,700 free blacks living in the area around Jerusalem, Virginia. A few were independent farmers, but most worked for white farmers in return for a few dollars and a shack in which to live. Because their living conditions were not much removed from the conditions that they had endured when they had been slaves, the depression was harder on these free blacks than it was on the poorer white farmers.

One of the farmers who was hit hard by the depression was Benjamin Turner's son, Samuel. Forced to choose between selling his slaves or getting more profit out of them, Samuel hired an overseer to drive them harder. Among his slaves was Nat, whom Samuel had inherited from his father.

Nat promptly ran away. Patrols and hunting dogs were sent out to find him, and they combed the nearby swamps and woods. However, Nat was nowhere to be found.

Nat's fellow slaves prayed for him. After two weeks had passed, the slaveowners gave up their search. The slaves rejoiced in secret.

Yet they were all in for a surprise 30 days later, when Nat, who had eluded all of his pursuers, walked up to the front porch of his owner's house and gave himself up. The other slaves were furious with him. Why did he come back when he had gotten away clean? they wanted to know. Why did he turn himself in? These were good questions, but he did not give them an answer.

However, Nat later wrote in his *Confessions* that while he was in hiding, "the Spirit" had chastised him for having his wishes directed to the things of this world and not to the "Kingdom of Heaven." One way to interpret this statement is that he realized his destiny was not only to pursue his own freedom but the freedom of his people. He had bigger plans and a greater destiny than a simple escape. Thus, he chose to sacrifice his own freedom—just as he was to sacrifice his life—so that his people might have a chance to fight for their freedom.

Samuel Turner was so amazed to see a runaway slave return of his own free will that Nat went unpunished. He returned to his daily work—plotting, dreaming, biding his time. But now, at least, he was a young man who had a sense of what his mission was.

People often develop an interest in religion during hard times, and as the economic depression continued, many of Nat's fellow slaves turned to religion for comfort. In the rural areas of the South, camp meetings and religious revivals became very popular. Whites gathered in huge tent cities to take part in days of preaching, feasting, singing, and expressing their religious convictions. The staid, respectable English church (both the Episcopal and the Anglican church), with its polite hymns and solemn ceremonies, had become outdated. Americans wanted a fiery religion, with hell and damnation, shouting, moaning, speaking in tongues—and even the handling of snakes, and new churches began to spring up all over the South.

Many slaves found solace from their labors at loud, boisterous religious revival meetings. During one of these meetings, Turner received the first of his divine revelations, and he soon became convinced that it was his mission to lead his fellow slaves to the "Kingdom of Heaven," his phrase for freedom.

American slaveowners were fearful that invading British troops would be successful in inspiring wide-scale slave rebellions during the War of 1812. The uprisings never took place, and some blacks, such as these riflemen at the Battle of New Orleans, fought with the Americans.

The slaveowners wanted to share their Christian religion with the slaves—adapted to suit their own purposes, of course. They hired preachers to explain to the slaves that the slaves who were patient on earth would get their reward in Heaven. If a slave was whipped, worked to death, or separated from his family, he would only be that much happier in Heaven, where he would be united with his family at last.

The slaveowners hoped that the slaves would believe these explanations. Perhaps some slaves did believe them and looked forward to Heaven, figuring that the white slaveowners would all go to Hell for their sin of slavery. But for the most part, the slaves adapted the religion of their owners to meet their own ends. They studied the Old Testament, learned about Moses leading the Jews out of slavery in Egypt, and took a special interest in the stories about Judgment Day.

The slaves created their own churches, where they were able to gather among themselves away from the view of whites. In these churches, they not only practiced religion, for they were religious people, much like their owners, but also dreamed of freedom and discussed the many rumors and hopes that often swept through the countryside.

Most of these rumors concerned the British. The slaves were always hoping that the former rulers of the American colonies would go to war against the United States. Most slaves wanted the British to take control of America because the British often talked about abolishing slavery (they would ultimately do so in 1834).

During the War of 1812, the British had promised freedom to all of the slaves who were willing to rebel against their American masters. Although the opportunity never arose for the slaves to take advantage of this offer, they did not forget it. Consequently, the slaves in Virginia hoped that the British would again attempt to invade the United States, much as they had done toward the end of the War of 1812. When the possibility of a British invasion or some other way of fighting for freedom was discussed during a religious service, this talk was often couched in phrases from the Bible—such as "Day of Judgment," "crossing over Jordan," and "coming of the Jubilee"—just in case whites were listening or had sent spies.

One version of Judgment Day came to Nat and his family in the early 1820s, shortly after he was married. Not much is known about Nat's wife. Her slave name was Cherry, she lived on the Turner farm, and her husband trusted her with his most secret plans and papers. After his slave rebellion, she was beaten and tortured in an attempt to get her to reveal his plans and whereabouts. Although we cannot know for sure, it is probable that Nat never mentioned her in his *Confessions* because he wanted to spare her and their three children as much pain as possible.

In 1822, soon after Nat was married to Cherry, Samuel Turner died. His estate had to be divided up, and so his property had to be appraised. Nat, his wife, their children, his mother (as well as his grandmother—if she was still alive), and the other slaves on the Turner farm were lined up with the cows and tools and furniture. A few appraisers went down the line assigning a value to each lamp, each chair, each tool, and each human being (we can only imagine how this very common Virginia practice affected Nat).

Nat was valued at $400, the going price for a top field hand. Cherry was valued at only $40.

Then Nat and his family were treated as if they were nothing more than chickens or hogs. The family was separated. Nat's mother was told to stay with Samuel Turner's daughter on the Turner farm, while

Nat was sold to one farmer and his wife was sold to another.

Although this division of the family surely must have been painful, it could have been worse. Nat's new owner, Thomas Moore, was a neighbor of Giles Reese, who had become the owner of Nat's wife and his children. Also, Nat was lucky not to be sold either south or west, where strong black men were being shipped daily to work on cotton, hemp, and turpentine plantations to replace the laborers there who were literally being worked to death. Life in Southampton County for a slave was difficult, but it was not quite as harsh as life on those plantations.

Nevertheless, the daily toll of work—as well as the sorrow and the humiliation of slavery—was still hard on Nat and all of his fellow slaves. Yet he did not dwell on these topics. He saw himself as a man of destiny, and he not only dreamed of his own independence but of freedom for all of his people. ◆

A tragic and all-too-common fate for slave families was to be split up when a master died and his possessions were divided among his heirs. The death of Turner's master in 1822 resulted in Turner being separated from his wife, Cherry, and their children.

4

"PROPHET NAT"

WHILE NAT TURNER slaved for Thomas Moore, he devoted his life to religion—or so it seemed. In fact, he was planning his rebellion.

From 1825 to 1830, Turner served as a preacher because it gave him the ability (at least on Sundays) to travel around the neighborhood. He preached at different black churches: at the Turner chapel which his former master had built for his slaves, at the Barnes Church on the North Carolina line, and at churches in Jerusalem and nearby Greensville County.

Often fasting during the week, Turner studied and prayed when he was not working, keeping himself apart from others. "I studiously avoided mixing in society, and wrapt myself in mystery," he said. On Sundays, he used a resonant voice filled with poetry to share his visions with the other slaves. His visions were of conflict, struggle, and liberation.

"I saw white spirits and black spirits engaged in battle," he cried out from the pulpit. "And the sun was darkened—the thunder rolled in the heavens and the blood flowed in streams—and I heard a voice saying, 'Such is your luck, such are you called to see, and let it come rough or smooth, you must surely bear it.' "

Turner prepared his followers for an uprising by preaching to them that "the great day of judgment was at hand." Some of his impassioned sermons were delivered at the Southampton Methodist Church (shown here).

Turner told his congregation that while he was working in the fields, he saw figures drawn in blood on the leaves. He interpreted this vision for his eager listeners as "the Blood of the Savior, who was about to lay down the yoke he bore for the sins of men." According to Turner, his vision meant that "the great day of judgment was at hand."

Turner soon became the most sought after of all the black preachers for miles around. His fellow slaves knew what he meant by sin, they knew what he meant by judgment, and they knew what he meant by salvation. Freedom was on all of their minds.

A few whites also understood what Turner was talking about. Although Sally Moore, his new owner's wife, had known him for years and thought that he was docile, her brother Salathial warned her that Turner was "a negro of bad character" who was stirring up trouble. Other whites suspected him of being a "conjure man," or witch doctor, and wished that the Moores would keep him closer to home.

Yet the Moores believed that he was harmless. Turner was polite and respectful, if just a little bit reserved and distant. He did not drink, steal, or gamble. He knew everything that there was to know about farming, and he worked like a mule all week. So they let him enjoy his preaching.

The slaves held "Prophet Nat" in so much respect that it bordered on awe. His dedication and single-mindedness gave them confidence in his ability and judgment. Rural Virginians—both blacks and whites—were simple people in superstitious times, and they came to believe that Turner was a prophet who could cure ailing people just with his touch. Some people even thought that he was so magical that he could control the weather.

Turner's eloquence and conviction were so impressive that he convinced a white man, E. T. Brantley, to give up his wicked ways and converted the

man to Methodism. Brantley even asked Turner to baptize him—an unheard-of thing in such bigoted times. Although the Methodist church refused to approve the baptism of a white man by a black slave, the two men went ahead and made plans to perform the ceremony at a river.

Word of this event spread for miles around, and on the day of Brantley's baptism, a crowd gathered on the bank of the river and threatened Turner and Brantley. It must have taken much courage for both of them to defy the menacing racism of the hostile and curious mob, yet they proceeded with the ceremony. They waded into the river, and Turner baptized Brantley while the crowd hooted and jeered.

Turner worked hard as a preacher. One Sunday he was in Jerusalem, the next in Cross Keys, the next in Bethlehem Crossroads or Bellfield. During his travels, he always made sure to take a different route and visit with a different family until he knew every swamp,

One of the places at which Turner preached was the village of Cross Keys. While traveling to his Sunday services, he learned which slaves he could trust with his plans for a slave revolt.

In 1822, the revolutionary black leader Denmark Vesey plotted a massive rebellion among slaves in Charleston, South Carolina. The attempt failed when an informer betrayed the rebels shortly before the uprising was set to take place.

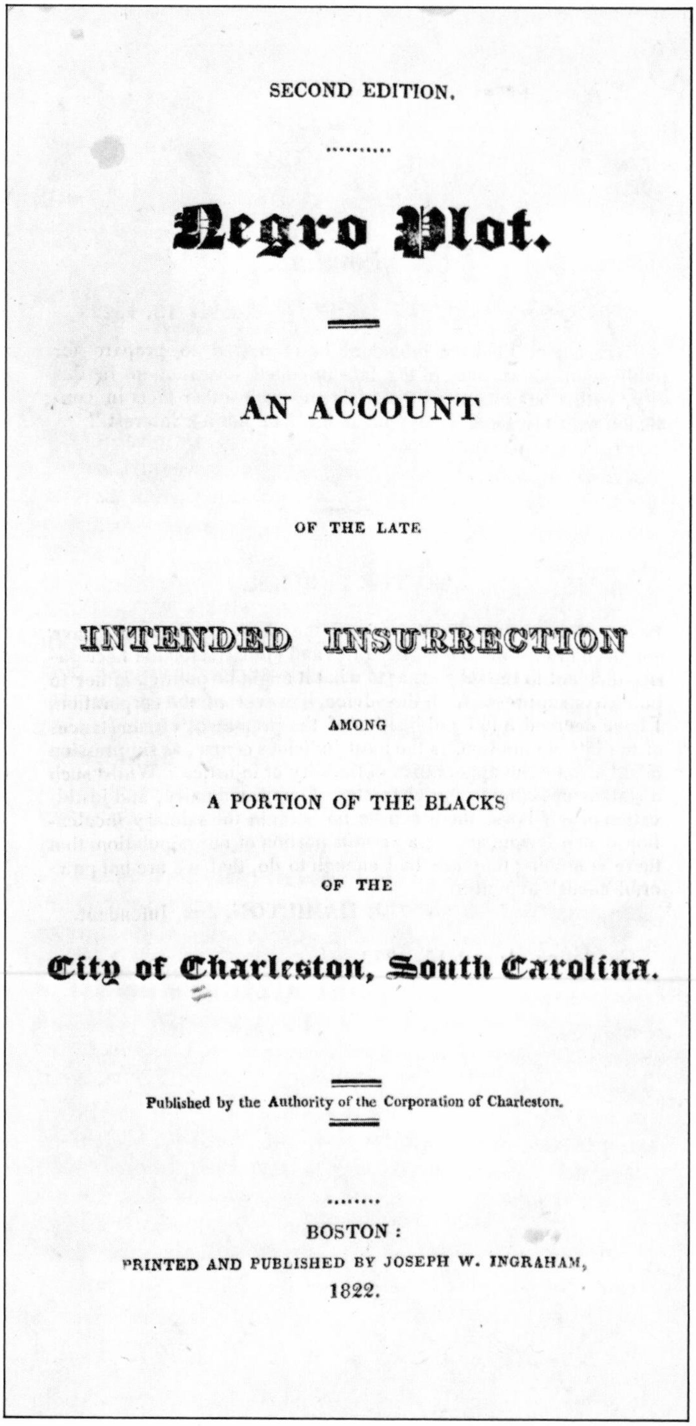

SECOND EDITION.

....

Negro Plot.

—

AN ACCOUNT

OF THE LATE

INTENDED INSURRECTION

AMONG

A PORTION OF THE BLACKS

OF THE

City of Charleston, South Carolina.

Published by the Authority of the Corporation of Charleston.

. . . .

BOSTON :

PRINTED AND PUBLISHED BY JOSEPH W. INGRAHAM,

1822.

every thicket, every forest, every dirt road, path, barn, shack, shed, and house within 30 miles. He was nothing if not thorough.

In between preaching, planning, and working, Turner spent as much time as possible with his wife and children at the Reese farm. He got to know everybody in the area, both blacks and whites. He knew which whites were mean to their slaves and which ones were not. He knew which blacks were bold and which ones were not. And he knew who could be trusted and who was a betrayer, eager to curry favor with his master.

This last piece of information was particularly important because the two largest slave rebellions until that time had both been betrayed by other blacks. Gabriel Prosser's rebellion in Richmond had been doublecrossed by one of his own people, and in 1822, even more heartbreaking news for rebellion-minded slaves had come from Charleston, South Carolina. An immense slave uprising led by a free black named Denmark Vesey had been betrayed to the whites and had failed.

Vesey was not unlike Turner in that he learned how to read and write and eventually devoted his life to the liberation of his people. He struggled to convince them to stop taking the insults of the slave-owners and to consider themselves as men. The next step after convincing them of this was to organize a rebellion.

Vesey and his recruits made their plans in strict secrecy. At the stroke of midnight, six organized battle units were to seize the town, seal off the major roads, and kill the plantation owners in their houses. Then they would either seize Charleston or, if that seemed impossible, commandeer a ship in the harbor and sail for the black republic of Haiti. Vesey's chief lieutenant, an African "conjure man" named Gullah (Angola) Jack, gave all of the recruits a crab claw as

The revolt of African captives on the Spanish vessel Armistad was the most famous of the slave re-bellions that took place on board ships in the 19th century. The rebels won their freedom and were eventually allowed to return to Africa.

a good-luck token and a sign that the ancient African gods were watching over them.

The conspiracy was huge. Vesey had not only organized the free blacks in the town but also the slaves on the surrounding plantations, taking hundreds into his confidence. That was his mistake. Some of the house servants were loyal to their masters and gave away Vesey's plans.

Vesey was arrested along with 70 others, including a few whites who were helping because they also wanted to do away with the slave system. He and 35 others were hanged, while 37 more blacks were sent to a penal colony—and certain death—in the Caribbean. Vesey and his men went to their deaths with their heads held high, never revealing any of the details of their conspiracy.

When the rebellion was over, the slaveowners in South Carolina breathed easier. However, on Christmas Eve in 1825 and every night thereafter for six months, buildings in Charleston were torched, once again creating terror among the town's white residents.

News traveled swiftly among the slaves throughout the country, so it is very likely that Turner was familiar with Vesey's rebellion in Charleston and became determined to emulate his courage while avoiding his errors. Consequently, Turner moved very slowly and deliberately, and his efforts paid off in the end, for his slave rebellion was not only the biggest and bloodiest in American history, but it was the most unexpected. Very few whites suspected what was brewing around them. As a white survivor in the area later said, "Not one note of preparation was heard to warn the devoted inhabitants of woe and death."

In addition to the slaves who knew and trusted Turner in the late 1820s, there were nearly 1,750 free blacks living in Southampton County. Many were servants, farm laborers, and sharecroppers, but some were independent small farmers and craftsmen, much like the dissatisfied free blacks who plotted with Vesey. One of Turner's most trusted followers was Billy Artis, a free black who owned a 14-acre farm yet was married to a slave woman. He knew that without freedom for all of his people, his own individual freedom was a

The most militant of the white abolitionist leaders during the 1830s was William Lloyd Garrison, who began publishing his highly influential newspaper, the Liberator, eight months before Turner's rebellion. Slaveowners were infuriated with Garrison and accused him of trying to incite black uprisings in the South.

charade. Consequently, he decided to join Turner's rebellion.

While Turner was making his plans and gathering his forces, the same stirrings of freedom were being felt around the country and in other parts of the world. The abolitionist movement, which demanded that human slavery be outlawed, was beginning to grow into a national movement, although it would not reach its full strength until after 1830. The first and the most radical of the abolitionists were black, but many whites—especially in the North—joined the movement as time went on.

Among the better-known white abolitionists who were believers in human rights and equality were

William Lloyd Garrison, who edited *The Liberator*, one of the nation's most popular antislavery newspapers, and John Brown, who ultimately gave his life while fighting slavery. Almost 30 years after Turner led his rebellion, Brown led an armed group of black and white abolitionists who attempted to capture the federal arsenal at Harpers Ferry, Virginia.

There were many different types of abolitionists. Some were against slavery on moral grounds, while others were against it for political reasons. Some—like the armed bands that were organized to defend runaway slaves in the northern cities—believed in taking action against slavery; in many cases, they opened fire on southern slavecatchers and sent them packing. Other abolitionists only believed in "moral persuasion" and never broke the law or threatened violence against the slaveowners. Some combined both methods—such as the Quakers, who would hide escaped slaves but would refuse to fight.

Some whites were against slavery without advocating freedom for blacks or equal rights. Many of these whites simply thought it best to ship all of the blacks in America back to Africa. They hated slavery only because they saw that it was ultimately dangerous to the whites. Others felt as well that they did not want free blacks living in "their" America.

The most militant abolitionists, of course, were the slaves themselves. They took part in slave revolts in Martinique, Cuba, and Jamaica as well as in the United States. In the fall of 1826, a group of slaves that was being taken from Maryland to Georgia hijacked the slave ship *Decatur*, killed two crew members, and sailed for Haiti. They were eventually captured, but when the ship was brought into New York City's harbor, all but one of the captives escaped to freedom. In Alabama, fugitive slaves who built a fort in the swamps were finally subdued, but not be-

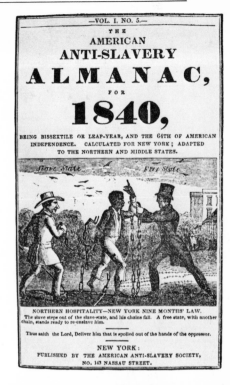

The American Anti-Slavery Almanac and other publications distributed by the northern abolitionist societies were banned in the South, but some contraband copies were smuggled in on ships.

fore the slaves, according to one report, had "fought like Spartans . . . and not one gave an inch of ground."

Echoing this militancy, the antislavery movement grew. Abolitionists spoke on the streets and in the churches in such northern cities as Boston, Massachusetts, and Philadelphia, Pennsylvania. However, abolitionists did very little campaigning against slavery in the South, where relatively few people were literate. Only people who knew how to read could be influenced by the abolitionists' published arguments. That is a major reason why slaves were not allowed to learn how to read and why it was a crime to teach reading to a slave. It is also why Turner's literacy was such an important aspect of his contribution to his people's struggle for freedom.

The governments of slave states such as Virginia did all that they could to keep abolitionist propaganda out of their states. The piece of literature that government officials hated the most—and the one that was perhaps an inspiration to Turner and other rebels around the country—was a book written by a free black abolitionist named David Walker. Originally published in Boston in 1829, *David Walker's Appeal to the Colored Citizens of the World, But in Particular, and Very Expressly, to Those of The United States of America* remains one of the most devastating, eloquent indictments of American slavery ever written.

In his *Appeal*, Walker called American slavery the cruelest and most hypocritical system that has ever existed because it dehumanizes its victims while flourishing in a so-called democracy. In particular, he had nothing but scorn for the white abolitionists who wanted to rid the country of blacks. "America is our country more than it is the whites," he said. "We have enriched it with our blood and tears."

Circulated chiefly by the author himself, Walker's *Appeal* was a direct call to his enslaved brethren in the South to strike boldly at their oppressors:

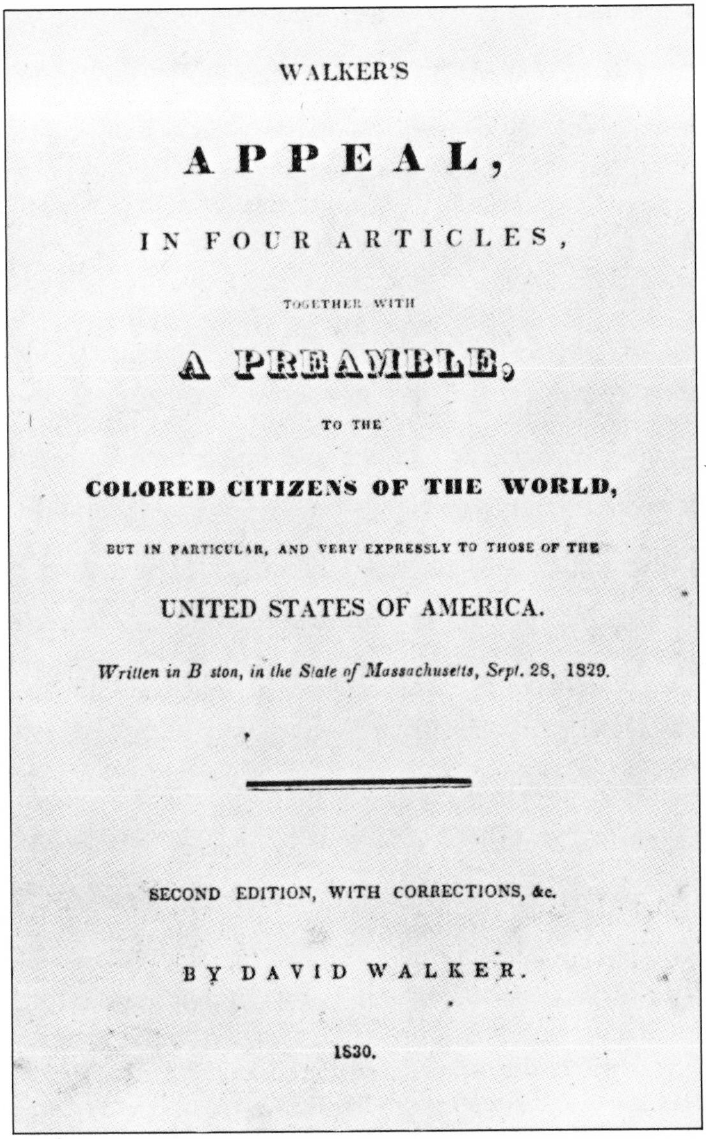

WALKER'S

A P P E A L ,

I N F O U R A R T I C L E S ,

TOGETHER WITH

A PREAMBLE,

TO THE

COLORED CITIZENS OF THE WORLD,

BUT IN PARTICULAR, AND VERY EXPRESSLY TO THOSE OF THE

UNITED STATES OF AMERICA.

Written in B ston, in the State of Massachusetts, Sept. 28, 1829.

————————

SECOND EDITION, WITH CORRECTIONS, &c.

BY DAVID WALKER.

1830.

Black abolitionist David Walker's antislavery pamphlet aroused a storm of controversy throughout America when it was published in 1829. His Appeal urged slaves to fight back against their oppressors and asked them, "Had you not rather be killed than be a slave to a tyrant?"

Should the lives of such creatures be spared? . . . Are they not the Lord's enemies? Ought they not to be destroyed? . . . If you commence, make sure work—do not trifle, for they will not trifle with you—they want us for their slaves, and think nothing of murdering us in order to subject us to that wretched condition—therefore, if there is an attempt made by us, kill or be killed.

During the 1820s, the Underground Railroad helped thousands of runaway slaves travel "freedom's road" to areas of relative safety in the North. However, for every refugee who escaped, many more were killed or recaptured.

This was strong talk by a skilled writer—indeed, one of the best of his day—and Walker's *Appeal* immediately sent shock waves of panic through the South. His book was promptly banned everywhere that slavery existed, and a price was put on his head. Walker died under mysterious circumstances only a year after his *Appeal* was published. It has been suspected that he was poisoned by friends of slavery in the North.

Walker's words soon proved to be a chilling foreshadowing of the fate of the slaveowners, who were killed by Turner and his men within two years of the publication of the *Appeal*. "They keep us miserable now," he said of the slaveowners, "and call us their property, but some of them will have enough of us by and by—their stomachs will run over with us; they want us for their slaves, and shall have us to their fill."

The words that so alarmed the slaveowners must have sounded like the pealing of a liberty bell to Turner. Although he never mentions Walker's book in his *Confessions*, the whites of Virginia never doubted that the hated *Appeal* contributed to Turner's rebellion. He might well have heard of it through word of mouth.

Yet Walker's words did not reach Virginia until almost the end of the 1820s, and Turner's course had been set several years before. During most of the years from 1825 to 1830, he was biding his time, waiting, trusting in the God in whom he sincerely believed: the God of judgment and salvation, who had promised him a sign.

Meanwhile, Turner continued his planning, getting to know the people, both black and white. Slowly and patiently, he was gathering his forces together, as a storm cloud gathers its energy for the lightning stroke that will illuminate both heaven and earth in one tremendous flash. ✺

5

"OURS IS
A FIGHT
FOR FREEDOM"

THE FIRST SIGN came on May 12, 1828. There was, as Turner later said, a "great noise" in the heavens. He stated that after this noise, "the Spirit instantly appeared to me and said the Serpent was loosened, and Christ had laid down the yoke he had borne for the sins of men, and that I should take it on and fight against the Serpent, for the time was fast approaching when the first should be last and the last should be first."

Other signs in the heavens would show Turner when to begin. He understood that after seeing these signs, "I should arise and prepare myself, and slay my enemies with their own weapons."

However, until these signs arrived, Turner kept this prophecy to himself. He prepared himself but withheld the details of his plans from even his closest and most trusted followers. He only slipped once, when he remarked to his owner, Thomas Moore, that the slaves would surely be free "one day or other." After hearing Turner say this, Moore beat him with a whip.

Later that same year, Moore died and Turner became the property of Moore's nine-year-old son, Putnam. Moore's widow, Sally, soon married Joseph Travis, a carriage maker from Jerusalem, who moved his business to the country and took up supervision of the farm, including all 17 slaves.

Entitled "Southern Industry," this engraving depicts a typical slave. Among the slaves and freedmen in Southampton County who were willing to sacrifice their lives for the chance to win their liberty with Turner were Hark Travis, Nelson Williams, Sam Francis, Henry Porter, Billy Artis, and Barry Newsome.

55

Turner continued working, keeping his mouth shut and his eyes open. He was looking for another sign. It came in February 1831, when a major eclipse of the sun took place. The eclipse was so striking and so unexpected that superstitious people of all races thought that the end of the world was at hand.

Turner, on the other hand, took this spectacular heavenly event as the sign he had been waiting for, and began to pull his plan together. He told his trusted inner circle to prepare their weapons, inform their contacts, and wait. The time to strike was approaching.

Turner had chosen for his inner circle about 20 people, all of whom he trusted completely. He chose so wisely and kept his secrets so well that today we only know the names of about seven or eight of his confidants. His wife, Cherry, was one. She was entrusted with maps written with pokeberry ink (made from a purple berry that grows wild in the South), lists in code, and strange ciphers that have never been deciphered to this day.

Hark, a slave at the Travis farm, was Turner's second in command. The name "Hark" was short for Hercules and was given to Turner's second because he was a giant. He looked like a "black Apollo," according to the whites.

Nelson Williams lived on the Williams farm, four miles southwest of Jerusalem. He was said to have special privileges—as Turner did—and was allowed to come and go as he pleased. A respected leader of the slaves, he was rumored by both blacks and whites to be a conjurer with supernatural powers.

Henry Porter and Sam Francis were said to be a bit more ordinary. Both lived near Turner and were reliable and well liked, although they apparently were not leaders. Henry Porter was one of 30 slaves on a good-sized plantation, and his task was to recruit for Turner among his fellow slaves. Sam Francis was owned

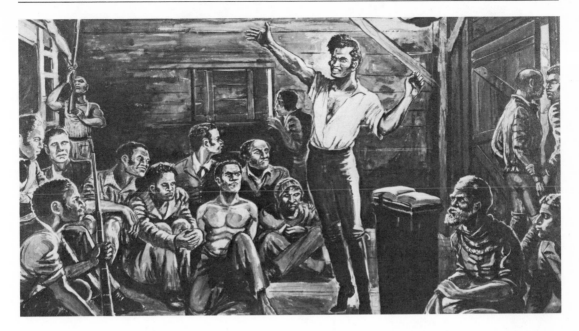

by Sally Travis's brother, so he had freedom of movement between the two farms.

Among the others whom Turner held in confidence were Billy Artis and Barry Newsome, two free black men in the neighborhood. Billy Artis was an independent farmer and—as he would ultimately show—a noble warrior. Not much is known about Barry Newsome except that Turner trusted him, which is a high enough recommendation for any man.

Turner began to meet and conspire in secret with these confederates. They compiled a list of 18 or 20 other trustworthy blacks. Most likely, they planned their route, tallying up the number of slaves and firearms, horses and mules on each plantation and farm between the Travis place and Jerusalem. This was the information Turner had spent years in gathering.

They set their target date for July 4, 1831, because it was a holiday. On that date, work was usually light and slaves were allowed to move around, while the whites were at ease or even drunk. Also, one suspects,

An eclipse of the sun in February 1831 was taken by Turner to be a sign from Heaven that he should begin plotting his rebellion. Gathering a group of trusted confederates, he told them of his visions of a world in which "the thunder rolled in the heavens, and blood flowed in streams."

Commonly subjected to brutal whippings and even maimings, some slaves were too terrified of their masters to join the front ranks of a liberation army. Turner hoped that once he established control of Southampton County, most of the area's slaves would rally to his cause.

the date was chosen for its ironic significance. As the black abolitionist and former slave Frederick Douglass was to point out later to the whites, "This is your holiday, not mine. You rejoice; we mourn."

Further arrangements were made. However, the rebels were frustrated in their efforts when Turner became sick as the fateful day drew near, and the rebellion was temporarily postponed. So many plans had been considered and rejected that, as he later explained, "it affected my mind." Perhaps his sickness was due to nervousness, fear, dread, anticipation; after all, the destiny for which he had been preparing for at least 10 years—and probably more—was about to come to pass.

Where did these doubts and fears come from? Surely Turner knew that he was taking on a well-armed and vicious enemy. Every slave uprising so far had failed and had been followed by mass hangings of black slaves. He was vastly outnumbered; even though Southampton County contained as many blacks as whites at that time, none of the blacks were armed and not all were willing to fight. They were psychologically unprepared, too. Many slaves believed that the whites were unbeatable, and Turner knew that it would take a few successes before significant numbers joined his rebellion.

The whites, on the other hand, were well prepared, even if they could be caught off guard. Slaveowners in Virginia told the world that their slaves were docile and content, but the slaveowners knew better than to believe their own propaganda. The Virginia militia was 10,000 strong, and there were numerous other volunteer military organizations. There were also the county patrols—the "paddy rollers" or "redlighters"—who rode the sandy roads with pitch pine torches pursuing runaways. Behind all this was the awesome power of the federal government, garrisoned at Fort Monroe in Norfolk.

To battle against this manpower, the slaves—disorganized, scattered, and unarmed—had only their desperation and desire for freedom. Also working against them was the knowledge that many revolts had been tried but none had succeeded. The always-present threat of betrayal and the need for secrecy meant that Turner's forces had to be kept extremely small—at least at the beginning, until after the first few blows had been struck.

All of these thoughts and more must have been going through Turner's mind, testing his determination, as the Fourth of July approached. We know from his *Confessions* that he was prepared to undergo the horrors of war and that he did not expect to survive ("Let it come rough or smooth, you must surely bear it," his vision had warned him). We also know that for several years he had sacrificed the meager family life that slavery allowed him, choosing instead to travel on his rare days of rest so that he could gather his forces and learn about the roads and the people around him.

A 13-year-old slave in Maryland at the time of the Southampton revolt, Frederick Douglass was deeply inspired by Turner's act of defiance. When Douglass later became an abolitionist newspaper editor in the North, he wrote, "We hold [slavery] to be a system of lawless violence; that it never was lawful and never can be made so."

Turner was certainly not a stonehearted fanatic. He was motivated by love—for his God, his family, and his suffering fellow blacks. He must have known even when he was playing with his two sons and his daughter (the children who were separated from him by slavery) that by fighting for their freedom, he would probably be igniting a holocaust around them—one that might consume them all. It is also likely that Turner's conscience was filled with David Walker's words: "I therefore ask the whole American people, had I not rather die, or be put to death, than to be a slave to any tyrant, who take not only my own, but my wife and children's lives by inches?"

Turner's hesitation in starting the rebellion is understandable. Yet his resolve was unshaken. Although July 4 came and went, the next and final sign came soon after.

On Saturday, August 13, there was such a strange darkness in the atmosphere that one could look directly at the sun. It seemed to shimmer and change colors—from green to blue to white. The phenomenon was visible along the entire eastern seaboard of the United States, and it made people fearful.

Then there was an even more awesome occurrence: A black spot appeared on the sun, passing slowly across its fiery surface. At this sign, Turner put his hesitations aside and called together his "chosen four": Hark Travis, Nelson Williams, Henry Porter, and Sam Francis.

"Just as the black spot passed over the sun," Turner told them, "so shall the blacks pass over the earth."

The word went out—cautiously but swiftly—to the other waiting slaves. The storm clouds began to gather. Only a few incidents, which were revealed later in the trials of the insurgents, gave any indication that something unusual was about to happen.

On the following Sunday morning, some whites who were passing a slave church near the boundary

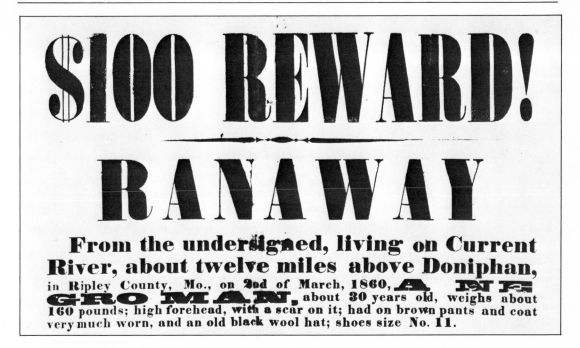

$100 REWARD!

RANAWAY

From the undersigned, living on Current River, about twelve miles above Doniphan, in Ripley County, Mo., on 2nd of March, 1860, A NEGRO MAN, about 30 years old, weighs about 160 pounds; high forehead, with a scar on it; had on brown pants and coat very much worn, and an old black wool hat; shoes size No. 11.

line between Virginia and North Carolina noticed that the slaves were more "disorderly" than usual. They were rapturously listening to a thunderous "hell and damnation" sermon. The preacher was Nat Turner.

On Monday, August 15, a slave girl overheard several slaves in a cabin on the Solomon Parker farm. She noticed that two of them were visitors from neighboring Sussex County. In low tones, they said, "If the black people come this way, we will join and kill the white people." One of the slaves said that he had had his ears cut off by his master and vowed that the man would find his own cropped in return before the year was out.

On Thursday, a slave named Isham told another slave, "General Nat is going to rise and murder all the whites." Blacks must join the revolt, Isham said, or the whites would win and then kill all of the slaves.

Later reports show that in Virginia and in North Carolina—in Southampton and in the neighboring counties—many of the slaves knew that something

Turner's rebels knew that the price of failure would be heavy. Those who escaped from vengeful companies of white militia would be hounded by notices advertising large rewards for the recapture of fugitives.

Because Turner and his fellow rebels kept their plans so well guarded, the whites in Southampton County had no inkling that a slave revolt was about to occur. The house shown here belonged to the county sheriff Clements Rochelle.

was about to happen. However, they were not (or claimed they were not) exactly sure of what it was or when it would take place.

When the rebels were put on trial later on, as a reign of white terror ravaged the countryside, many blacks were eager to show their loyalty to the whites by denouncing Turner. It must be noted, though, that before the rebellion took place, not a word was heard. Turner had planned well.

August seemed to be a good month for Turner and his men to strike. Because it was a time when the crops had already been planted and the harvest had not yet begun, everyone's workload was relatively light. And Sunday was the lightest workday of all. The slaves had time for hunting and fishing while the whites went to church and then drank apple brandy and visited neighbors and relatives for the rest of the day.

On the evening of Saturday, August 20, 1831, Turner laid down his farm tools for the last time. He told Hark to prepare a dinner for Sunday at Cabin Pond, in the woods at the back of the Travis place, and to bring together the "chosen four."

Perhaps Turner visited his family at the Reese farm on Sunday morning, secretly giving his children a final kiss and having a tearful farewell with his wife. He took his time joining his men, not wanting to seem too familiar to them. He had studied why the French emperor Napoleon and the liberator Toussaint L'Ouverture were successful leaders, and he knew that the authority of a leader was increased by a little mystery and aloofness.

On Sunday afternoon, at about three o'clock, Turner joined his men at Cabin Pond. He found them sitting around a fire, roasting a pig and sharing some apple brandy. There were Hark Travis and Nelson Williams, Henry Porter and Sam Francis, and two new recruits: Jack and Will, a slave owned by Nathaniel Francis. Turner knew Jack, but he was unsure of Will and challenged him: "How came you here?"

Will answered, "My life is worth no more than the others, and my liberty is as dear to me."

"Do you think to obtain it?"

"I will, or lose my life."

Satisfied with this answer, Turner welcomed him.

The men sat around the fire and made their final plans. They decided to strike that very night. They would begin with Turner's masters, the Travis family, relying on sheer terror and speed to give them the initial advantage.

According to black folklore, Turner gave a final speech to his men in which he laid out their strategy and goals. He said, "Remember, we do not go forth for the sake of blood and carnage; but it is necessary that, in the commencement of this revolution, all the whites we meet should die, until we have an army strong enough to carry out the war on a Christian basis. Remember that ours is not a war for robbery, nor to satisfy our passions; it is a struggle for freedom."

Turner warned them to "spare neither age nor sex." Then they all stood, doused the fire, picked up their weapons—at that point only hatchets and knives—and set out across the fields and through the woods on the bloody journey that would carry them into history. ☙

6

"GENERAL NAT"

AT TWO O'CLOCK in the morning on Monday, August 22, 1831, Turner and his band of men stood in the yard of the Travis house. They were joined by two other slaves, Austin and a teenager named Moses. They approached the house. Hark wanted to break through the door with his axe, but Turner held him back, worried that the noise might wake the nearest neighbor, whose house was less than a half mile away. The night was deep and silent, and Turner wanted to preserve the element of surprise as long as possible.

Hark fetched a ladder and placed it against the side of the house. Turner waved him and the other men aside and climbed it alone. It was important to him that he actually lead the way, at least at the beginning.

After a few breathless moments, when the only sounds in the yard were the crickets and the frogs in the distant ponds, the downstairs door was unbarred with a muffled thud and Turner's whisper came from the darkness inside: "The work is now open to you." The rebels poured into the house as silently as shadows, their knives and axes gleaming in the moonlight.

Turner began his revolt early in the morning of August 22, 1831. The rebels vowed that they would spare no white man, woman, or child on their march to the nearby town of Jerusalem.

With Will close behind him, Turner led the way to the upstairs bedroom, where Joseph Travis and his wife were sleeping. As the General, the Prophet, the leader of the rebellion, Turner knew that he must strike the first blow and draw first blood. He struck with a blunt sword, and the master of Travis farm screamed bloody murder. Will moved in from behind and finished off Travis and his wife before they were fully awake.

Downstairs, the other men began to kill the rest of the whites in the house—one of them being 12-year-old Putnam, Turner's legal master. Soon all in the house were dead but an infant, momentarily forgotten in its cradle. Remembering Turner's instruction to "spare neither age nor sex," Henry Porter and Will returned upstairs and killed the child.

After the screams and blows, there was silence once again. But now there was also the smell of blood,

The rebels carried out their grisly work with ruthless efficiency, making sure that they left no survivors who could spread an alarm. This old woodcut illustration depicts the massacre of the Travis family and the fight with John Barrow.

dark and sticky, on the plank floor. Jack was sick to his stomach in the yard. Moses grew afraid, but he followed the others anyway. Both were learning that freedom can carry a great and awful price.

From the Travis house, they took four rifles, several old muskets, and some gunpowder. Leading his men to the barn, Turner armed them and drilled them with the weapons, marching them up and down to impress on them the fact that they were not outlaws or bandits but soldiers—soldiers of their people.

The next farm that they reached belonged to Sally Travis's brother, Salathial. It was he who had warned her that Turner was not just an innocent and carefree preacher, and tonight his fears were to be fully justified. Henry Porter and Will knocked on the door, telling the man that they had a letter for him. When he opened the door, he was pulled outside into the yard and was cut down.

In perfect silence and order, the rebels marched on, toward the town of Jerusalem more than 10 miles away. Turner had ordered that no firearms were to be used as of yet. Either at Salathial Francis's or along the way, he obtained a light sword, which he carried as a symbol of his command.

At the next darkened farmhouse, an old woman and her son were killed. As Turner later said in his *Confessions*, the son awoke during the rebels' attack, "but it was only to sleep the sleep of death, he had only time to say, 'who is that?' and he was no more."

Another house was passed by because its owner saw them coming and barricaded himself inside. "Here I am, boys!" he dared them. "I will not go from my home to be killed." Turner decided that the house was not worth attacking; the noise of the battle would arouse the neighbors. Instead, the rebels raced on toward town, picking up more slaves at every stop.

The first shots were fired near dawn, when it was no longer possible to catch people asleep in their beds. Ironically, these shots came at the old Turner place, where the slave revolt leader had lived for 10 years. The farm was now a plantation with 18 slaves. The overseer was taken by surprise at the cider press and was shot lest he warn the people in the house.

However, the shot proved to be enough of a warning. Widow Turner and a visiting neighbor tried to lock themselves inside the kitchen, but their efforts were of no use. The door was bashed down with an axe and both women were killed.

By the time that daylight came and the other white slaveowners were beginning to wake up, the rebels had become a full company of 15 armed men, 9 of them mounted. Turner split up his forces, sending 6 men to one farm and 9 to another. At each farm, what he later called "the work of death" was gruesome. However, the rebellion had not yet turned into a full-fledged fight. The rebels still had the advantages of speed and surprise.

Turner discovered that his sword was too dull for fighting, but he continued to carry it anyway. There were plenty of fighters now, and they were as eager as he and far more skilled.

At every homestead, all of the whites were killed without exception and all of the slaves who were willing to join the fight were recruited. Those who had no stomach for the rebellion were warned not to betray or interfere with it in any way. Then each house was searched for firearms, ammunition, food, clothing, and money. Horses and mules were saddled and taken. There was no petty individual looting, and in no instance were individuals humiliated or tortured, nor were women molested or raped.

The only lapse in the discipline of Turner's army was brought about by the apple brandy that was found in every Southampton home. Even though Turner was never known to drink, he initially permitted his men to imbibe at every stop. In doing so, he allowed a thief into the army's ranks—one that would eventually steal the men's resolve. However, this problem was not to surface until later on.

Francis. Travis. Whitehead. Bryant. Newsome. The homesteads fell one by one as the rebels rode toward Jerusalem, destroying the slaveowners farm by

While ransacking the farms of their masters, Turner's soldiers collected muskets that they would need to fight against well-armed militia companies. Most of the guns that they found were in poor condition.

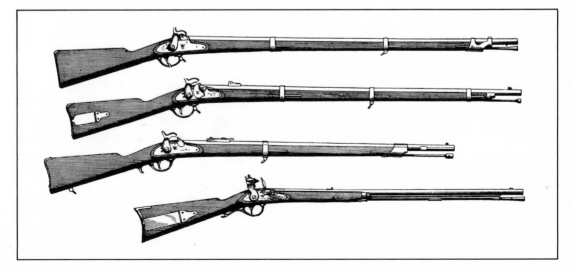

The house owned by Giles Reese was one of the few places that the rebels spared during their march. Turner's wife and three children were slaves on Reese's farm.

farm. The Giles Reese place, where Turner's wife lived, was spared, as was the farm of a childhood friend, John Clark Turner. But virtually no other homesteads were spared from an attack. It was a fearsome kind of war, swift and bloody and remorseless.

Turner split up his forces again, sending the cavalry with Hark. Upon arriving at the Porter farm with half of his army, he found that the place was empty. Everyone had fled. Turner understood immediately that word about the rebellion was out. The rebels had now lost the advantage of surprise (as he knew they would sooner or later).

Next, Turner and his men reached a strategic objective, the Barrow farm, and found the owner, a veteran of the War of 1812, hoeing in the fields. The old man fought so valiantly before he was killed that the rebels honored him by wrapping his body in a quilt and placing a plug of tobacco on his chest—this was the way that warriors were honored in parts of Africa. Barrow was the only one of their enemies that the rebels so honored. In contrast, when some of the rebels were killed later on, their bodies were mutilated shamelessly by their enemies.

By this time, Turner was riding at the back of his army, trying to coordinate the whole as his men struck from farm to farm. Billy Artis, Will, Hark Travis, and Nelson Williams had come to the forefront as natural leaders; they were Turner's lieutenants. Hark was the first among them, leading the largest detachment of cavalry.

At about 10 A.M., Turner caught up with a section of his forces at the Harris farm, only five miles from the town of Jerusalem. Their journey was half over.

As Turner rode up to them, his sword in hand, he was surprised to see how large his forces had grown. Forty insurgents, all mounted—and many of them armed with rifles or muskets—greeted him with loud hurrahs. Forty black warriors with African blood— an army of slaves riding for freedom, honoring their modern-day Spartacus (a leader of a slave rebellion in ancient Rome).

This was Turner's greatest moment, the culmination of his dreams and plans. Win or lose, he had achieved something that no other slave in America had ever accomplished: He had put together a slave army, mounted and armed and in the field, fighting for its freedom. Now they would show their owners how they could fight!

Some of the men had been drinking, though, and this worried Turner. He sternly ordered his troops away from the brandy barrels that they had rolled onto the lawn and told them to stand at attention. Then he dressed them down. He explained again that they were fighting for a cause beyond their individual freedom or pleasure, and in his magnificent preacher's voice, he commanded them to "shape up."

At this point, Turner's authority was challenged for the first time. A slave named Aaron spoke up and warned that it was time to turn back, that the rebellion did not have a chance against the white man's powerful forces.

Nonsense, Turner said. Even though the slaves were outnumbered, they could defeat the whites if enough slaves rallied to their cause.

Aaron persisted. He said that he had accompanied his master to fight in the War of 1812, and if Turner had seen as many white soldiers as Aaron had seen at Norfolk, then Turner would know better.

History has not recorded Turner's reply, much less his feelings. Certainly, he knew that there was much truth in what the fainthearted slave was saying. Half of Virginia was already up in arms and was preparing to crush the rebels. And if Virginia failed, the full strength of the United States would be brought to bear against them.

Yet Turner knew that there was no turning back. They were facing an enemy that refused to recognize their humanity, much less their right to rebel, and there was no thought of quarter or surrender. A few individuals might slip back to their slave cabins, but the leaders were known. Besides, win or lose, they had already struck a mighty blow against slavery— an army of black rebels would be an inspiration to future generations, even in defeat. Were they not free men now, if only for a day? Was it not better to die free than to live in slavery?

While Turner knew all of this, he probably knew as well that no general ever rallied his troops by preparing them for defeat. So he may have attempted to inspire his men by invoking words similar to those of David Walker's: "I think one black man is worth fifty whites. Unleash us and you have unleashed tigers." Or perhaps he drew on the history that his mother had been so careful to instill in him, reminding his men about their heritage as Africans; they were the sons of great warriors.

Harsh, scornful, soaring, bitter, poetic—whatever words Turner used, they ended the debate. The doubter was silenced, if not converted, and the general prevailed.

Yet the men who followed Turner were inspired not only by their leader's oratory but by what was in their hearts. Many of them were teenagers who would be facing a life of servitude if they gave up the fight. They knew how powerful and ruthless their enemy was, just as surely as they knew that they were fighting for a freedom that could not easily be won.

As the rebels stood in the ranks with their guns at the ready, they must have known the literal meaning of the words "freedom or death." Each man had to make a choice in his heart. He had to choose between riding with Turner, even into the jaws of death, or slipping back into a life of slavery, which was to kill them, as David Walker said, "by inches."

Almost to a man, they chose to follow Turner.

A final hurrah was shouted, and then Turner, with a gruff command, formed up his ranks. Then his army rode off, toward the next slaveowner's farm.

A map of the southeastern quarter of Virginia shows the area affected by Turner's revolt. The insurgents' march began at the Travis farm, a short distance southwest of Jerusalem.

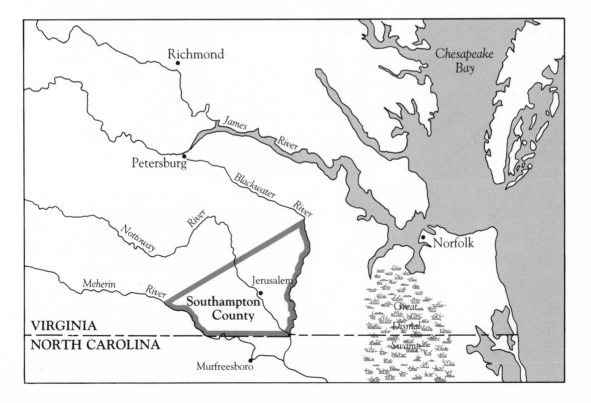

As word of Turner's rebellion spread throughout the Virginia countryside, both whites and blacks began to make speculations about where the rebel commander was intending to lead his army. Some believed that he planned to establish a base of resistance in the nearby Great Dismal Swamp.

The general continued to ride at the rear rather than the front of his troops—planning, watching, looking for signs. He knew that the going would get rougher, not easier. So far there had been little resistance. But sooner or later, the whites would stop fleeing in terror and confusion. They would rally together, and then his army would face a fight.

Until the whites started to band together, the raids continued to go smoothly. Turner adapted his tactics to fit the size of his growing army. He placed his fastest, fiercest-looking troops at the front of the column because he wanted to terrorize the whites into fleeing. The more people who saw the rebels coming, the more fear was generated.

At each homestead, the rebels charged ahead with their guns blazing and their axes flashing while shouting out their battle cries. The pattern was the same at each homestead. There was a charge, shooting, screams—and then silence.

The deeds were already done by the time Turner reached the house. The whites had been killed—men, women, and children alike. The weapons and powder had been seized. The horses had been saddled, and more men had been mounted. Then, at a sign from the general, the army would ride on toward Jerusalem.

More slave recruits joined at every farm—the strongest and boldest of the men and boys. Although it has not been recorded that any women rode with the force, they joined in the fighting at every plantation. By noon, the rebel army was 60 strong.

They began to ride openly through the fields. The element of surprise had gone with the darkness; now, speed was all. If they could gain the town of Jerusalem, they would at least be relatively secure until more slaves joined them. And then . . .

But they would let the future take care of itself. Perhaps they would flee for the Great Dismal Swamp, 20 miles to the east. Perhaps they would fight their way to the sea and hijack a ship for Haiti. Perhaps they could drive the whites from this corner of Virginia altogether. Consciously or not, Turner must have always had this last possibility in his mind, for he strictly forbade his men to burn or destroy any house or barn. His army destroyed only the people but left the livestock, houses, and barns, as though the rebels hoped that they might someday return to occupy them.

And why not? Had not they built every house, laid every fence rail, plowed and cleared every field? Whose land was it, if not theirs? **◆**

7

THE
FORTUNES
OF WAR

SLAVE REBELLION! It was mid-morning on Monday, August 22, 1831, and southeastern Virginia was in a state of panic. Riders with news of the rebellion had reached Jerusalem, and the church bells were tolling the alarm. Terrified families were straggling into town across the Nottoway River, and the streets were choked with refugees. In Sussex and Greensville counties to the north and west, in North Carolina to the south, slaves were seen literally jumping for joy, kicking their heels in the air at the roadsides. It had come, as everyone in their heart of hearts had known it would someday—the long-awaited, or long-dreaded (depending on one's point of view) Judgment Day. Jubilee. Slave rebellion!

Rumors flashed through the air like summer lightning: The British had landed and were on their way; an army of 500 slaves was riding down on Jerusalem. Through it all, however, a few people learned the truth, and the truth was terrifying enough for the whites and joyous enough for the blacks. Nat Turner, Southampton County's own "Prophet Nat," was leading a slave army toward the town, leaving a zigzag trail of death and destruction behind him.

Amid all of the confusion in Jerusalem, Justice James Trezevant of the Southampton County Court scrawled a hasty note: "Terrible insurrection; several families obliterated. Send arms and men at once; a

Slowed by their consumption of too much apple brandy, the rebels delayed their attempt to seize the stores of weapons and ammunition in Jerusalem. They soon found their way blocked by large forces of white militia.

large force may be needed." The judge sent the message with a fast rider, who clattered across the boards of the Nottoway Bridge, heading north toward Petersburg and Richmond.

All of the church bells in Jerusalem were tolling in warning as lone riders, nervously looking out for armed blacks, galloped through the countryside to alert the scattered militia. Meanwhile, women and children barricaded themselves in the stores and churches, and men rolled out cider barrels, cotton bales, boards, and logs to build a hasty barricade at the bridge over the Nottoway River, all the while scanning the Murfreesboro Road for the army of 500 slaves that was rumored to be coming.

By noon, the rebel army that they feared was only three miles from Jerusalem. Behind them was a trail of death and terror, with more than 50 whites killed and the buzzards still circling. At the Waller plantation, where there had been a school, 10 children

On the day after the outbreak of the rebellion, horseback riders were carrying news about Turner's army to places as far away as Richmond, the capital of Virginia (shown here as it appeared at the end of the Civil War).

had been killed and thrown into a pile, as if in terrible revenge for all of the innocent black babies thrown from the slave ships to the sharks.

Some of the rebels, like Billy Artis, wept at the sight of the slain children. But not Turner. He viewed it all, as he was to say later, with "silent satisfaction," knowing that unrelenting terror was his only hope of scattering the whites and winning freedom for his fellow slaves. He had held his army back from attacking people whom he did not know well only once, at a cabin belonging to poor whites who held no slaves. They were people, he said, "who thought no more of themselves than they did the negroes," and therefore they were not subjected to his army's terrible retribution.

More ominous to Turner than the slaughter was the brandy. He could see that he had been too lax, and the alcohol was now taking its toll on his men in spite of his efforts to curb their drinking. Although

Jacob Williams's farm was the scene of one of the bloodiest slaughters carried out by the rebels. Some slaveowners were luckier and managed to flee from their homes shortly before the arrival of Turner's army.

Turner did not know about it at the time, one of the rebels who got drunk and fell behind was captured and then tortured and mutilated by whites.

By this time, the slaveowners had rallied, spread the alarm, and were beginning to fight back, although they were still a bit disorganized. There were two bands of militia in the field, separated and unaware of each other. One group, numbering 30 or 40 men, was led by a Jerusalem lawyer in his thirties named William C. Parker. Another group of about 20 men was led by Captain Arthur Middleton of the Southampton Militia. Both groups were following Barrow Road.

Middleton's group reached the Waller school only minutes after the slaughter there, and Middleton was so shaken by what he saw that he deserted the company and rode off to find his own family. Two other men, Alexander Peete and James Bryant, took command and rode on cautiously, looking for the slave army. It was they who found Turner's drunken soldier straggling behind in the road. They cut the tendons in his heels and left him unable to stand or walk. When another group came by, the men tied him to a tree and used him for target practice.

The retaliation of the whites—as savage as anything that Turner's army did—was already beginning.

At a little after noon on Barrow Road, Turner could see smoke from the town over the trees and hear the frantic ringing of the church bells. He formed up his men, and they started riding full speed, straight toward Jerusalem. He knew that by now there were companies of militia out looking for him. Although his men were well mounted, their weapons were poor and there was little ammunition. They had powder but only a little birdshot. So Turner showed them how gravel, poured down the barrel of a gun, would serve almost as well as lead.

Scores of slaves rushed to join the avenging army of "General Nat." Four people were killed at the house owned by Rebecca Vaughan, one of the last places attacked by Turner's band.

Turner knew that the success of his rebellion depended on gaining the town. In Jerusalem, there were arms, ammunition, and food. The whites, he knew, were panicked and terrorized to the point that they could be driven out. He hoped that once he and his men were established in the town, they could hold out long enough for larger numbers of slaves to join them, or perhaps even until the still-hoped-for intervention of the British.

It was at the Parker farm on Barrow Road, in what came to be known as the Battle of Parker's Field, that Turner faced the open fighting he had both dreaded and sought. His inexperienced and poorly armed men were to do better than he had expected.

The battlefield was not of Turner's choosing but was forced on him by the fading discipline of his soldiers. They were riding toward the town, with Turner at the rear, when they passed the Parker farm, where several of the men had relatives and friends among the slaves. Over the protests of Hark and the other leaders, the men stopped and went out back to the slave cabins to recruit more fighters—and to show off their guns and horses.

When Turner caught up with Hark, he was furious. He could hear the church bells, and he knew that the whites were gathering their forces. Angry and impatient, he left eight men by the gate to guard the front of the house and rode down the hill with Hark to the slave cabins to fetch the rest. What he saw there dismayed and sickened him: Several of his men were drunk on apple brandy, and others were bragging and showing off—when there was a war to be fought! Angrily, Turner ordered them back into formation when he heard the ominous sound of gunshots coming from the front of the house.

While Turner had gone to fetch the men from the slave quarters, the militia force of 20 men led by Peete and Bryant had come over the hill and surprised the 8 men left standing guard. Although the rebels

fought back, their ancient, single-shot guns that took a half minute to load were not much good against 20 modern military rifles. As Turner's guard fell back, the slaveowners' militia advanced on the house, thinking victory was in their grasp.

Seeing that the men around him were wavering and indecisive, Turner ordered them into battle formation and brought them around the house, into the high weeds in the field. Gaining strength from his confidence, the men followed—guns, knives, and axes at the ready.

The whites kept on advancing until Turner yelled, "Charge! Fire on them!" Yelling and screaming, the rebel army leaped into action, inspired by their leader's courage. The militia hesitated, then broke ranks and fell back in panic and disorder. These men had never seen black slaves with weapons before. Captain Bryant's horse stampeded, and he was carried away, into the woods and out of the battle.

Yelling wildly, brandishing axes and swinging gun butts, the insurgents chased the slaveowners' militia over the hill. But just then their fortunes changed.

The poorly armed rebels put up a valiant fight against the militia units, but they were finally overwhelmed at the Battle of Parker's Field and forced to fall back. The site of the battle is shown here.

Turner hoped to use the Cypress Bridge to cross the Nottoway River and then attack Jerusalem. To his disappointment, he found that the bridge was already guarded by a squad of militiamen.

One of the other groups of militia happened to be passing on the road, purely by chance, and it reinforced the fleeing whites, giving them time to reload their weapons. Regrouping while doubling in numbers, the militia counterattacked, and this time it was the rebels' turn to fall back, their guns discharged and useless.

In the withering fire of the militia's better weapons, five of Turner's best men fell wounded. Others panicked and fled into the woods. Hark's horse was shot out from under him, but Turner caught another mount on the fly and handed the reins to Hark. The two men then led a retreat into the thick forests along the Nottoway River, carrying their wounded with them. They knew what would happen to any men whom they left behind.

Stopping as soon as they were safe in the woods, Turner rallied his troops. A few stragglers joined them, bringing their force back up to 20. The men were shaken; many were bleeding. Others, the survivors said, were still hiding in the woods or fleeing across the fields.

Turner was still bound to try to take Jerusalem, which he believed was his best hope for success. By now it was clear that the main road was blocked by the militia; he had not expected so many men to arrive there so soon. But in his years of preparation, Turner had made other plans. He would cross the Nottoway at Cypress Bridge, three miles south of Jerusalem, and enter the town from behind.

Turner led his men through the brush, then down a little-known back road. But when they reached the bridge, his worst fears were realized. The little wooden span was bristling with guns and crawling with nervous, fierce-looking, armed whites. Turner's forces were too small to take it.

It was now in the late afternoon, and Turner had yet another plan. Riding fast, he and Hark led the men south, then doubled back north, across the Barrow Road again, eluding all pursuers. He was headed for the Ridley plantation—one of the largest in the county, with 145 slaves—where he hoped to recruit enough followers to make up his losses.

It was dusk by the time they reached the Ridley place, and again luck was against them. The militia had beat them there. The slaveowners had occupied and barricaded the main buildings and were keeping a close watch on the slaves.

Without letting the militia see them, Turner and Hark led their weary troops into the woods nearby, set up lookouts, and camped for the night. Their numbers were back up to 40; in spite of the guards at the Ridley place, 4 of the slaves had managed to sneak away and join them.

The men were exhausted, demoralized, and shaken by the defeat at Parker's field. More than anything, Turner knew, they needed rest. Tomorrow their fortunes might change. ✺

8
RETREATS
AND
REVERSES

◆◇◆

I T WAS MIDNIGHT. Turner had not been asleep for long when he was startled and awakened by what he later said was "a great racket." Getting up, he found some of his men mounted, some reaching for their weapons in the dark, and others scrambling about in confusion. One of the sentinels had given a warning cry, and the entire camp had fallen into disarray.

Turner suspected that it was a false alarm, yet he still sent scouts out to the edge of the woods to check up on the Ridley house. Sure enough, the militia was safely inside. They were not going to attack in the darkness.

But the damage was done; Turner's inexperienced force was already panicked. When the scouts returned, they were taken for attackers and fired on. Disorder fed on disorder, and in the ensuing confusion, many of the troops deserted.

Dawn found Turner without sleep, frustrated, low on ammunition and food, and down to 20 men again. Giving up on the idea of sleep, he ordered his men to mount. Hoping to gain recruits, they rode for the nearby Blunt plantation, where he knew there were 60 slaves.

In the gray dawn light, the place looked deserted. Turner thought that perhaps his luck was turning at last for the better: Perhaps all of the whites were with

By the morning of August 23, 1831, the rebels were in full retreat. Bands of vengeful slaveowners hunted down fugitives from Turner's army in the woods and marshes of Southampton County.

Repulsed at the Blunt plantation with heavy losses, the panicked rebels were soon scattered by white troops.

the militia at the Ridley house. Cautiously, the rebels rode through the gate, with Hark leading the way. Still cautious, Hark yelled out. There was no answer. Then he fired his gun into the air—

A thunderous volley of gunfire came from the house. It was an ambush! The horses and mules— farm animals that had been pressed into cavalry service—panicked and galloped wildly, carrying the rebels around and around the house while shotgun and rifle fire coming from behind the shutters picked them off. Hark fell, badly wounded. Horses tumbled and crushed their riders. Worst of all, some of Blunt's slaves joined in the fight on the side of their masters. Perhaps they were forced to fight; perhaps they fought willingly.

Shouting at his men to follow him, Turner retreated. This time he was forced to leave Hark and the other wounded men behind. Will helped him pull the troops back into some kind of order, and the small rebel army, exhausted and demoralized, backtracked through the woods. Many of them were wounded, most of them were without mounts, and some were without weapons.

At 10:00 A.M., they approached the Harris farm, where Turner's army had assembled and saluted their leader with bold and hopeful hurrahs only 24 hours before. However, this place, too, was crawling with whites—they were fresh troops with military rifles and horses. While Turner and his men were assessing the troops from the edge of the woods, a lookout spotted them. There was an alarm followed by shouts. Then came a blast of rifle fire, and three more of Turner's men fell dead. Among them was Will.

In response, the rebels knelt, aimed, and fired, and then turned to flee into the woods. Shouting, the militia set out after them. The skirmish in the woods was brief and bitter. The rebels, who were outnumbered, were outrun and then overwhelmed.

Turner was among the few who managed to escape, but this time he could not count on his forces to regroup. His army was in total disarray, with many dead or wounded and others scattered in every direction.

Unwilling to give up, Turner kept his sword, even though it was useless as a weapon. He found two men, then two more, and led them to a hiding place where they concealed themselves while the searching patrols almost stumbled over them. Finally, night fell around them, and, shivering and exhausted, the five men stumbled out of the woods onto a back road.

With his hand on his sword, Turner spoke softly but earnestly to inspire the men for one last try at freedom. Two of them, Curtis and Stephen, had joined the rebellion on the night before, sneaking away from the Ridley plantation, and were still fairly fresh. Turner sent them riding south, ordering them to round up as many men as they could and bring them to the woods at the Travis place, where the rebellion had begun. He would wait there for them. The revolt was not over, he insisted. They must not give up.

Accompanied by the other two men, both of them exhausted like himself, Turner struck off through the darkness. They made their way through the woods and along the back roads to the Travis place. While his two companions slept, Turner sat up all night and waited for his reinforcements to arrive.

The sun rose, but no one had come.

Turner then played his last card. He awakened his remaining two men and sent them out just as he had dispatched the others, instructing them to bring anyone whom they could find to Cabin Pond, where he had planned the revolt with his "chosen four." He would wait for them there.

They left, and he was never to see them again.

Although Turner had no way of knowing it, by this time half of his men had been killed and about

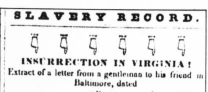

Turner's rebellion sent a shock-wave through America and opened many eyes to the bitter hatred that slaves felt for their oppressors. However, the Richmond gentleman whose account of the revolt was extracted in this Liberator article chose to view the revolutionaries as merely "deluded wretches."

half had been captured. Few had turned themselves in. Billy Artis had ridden from plantation to plantation, with his slave wife at his side, in a futile effort to rally support after the defeat at Blunt's. When he was at last chased down and surrounded, he defended himself with rifle fire instead of surrendering. After the shooting stopped and the whites moved in to inspect him, all they found was his hat on a stick, and his body. He had saved his last shot for himself.

Stephen and Curtis, Turner's first two messengers, had been captured less than a mile into their journey. They were taken to Cross Keys at gunpoint and locked in a log hut with other actual and suspected rebels. The little town was filled with refugees, and the whites were on a rampage. Some wanted the blacks held for trial; others wanted them beaten or executed on the spot. One female slave was tied to a tree and shot by her enraged owner.

By Tuesday, not only Southampton County but the entire state of Virginia was armed and out for blood. Judge Trezevant's message had arrived at the governor's mansion in Richmond at 3:00 A.M. on Tuesday, just as Turner was being awakened by the panic in the woods. Because the first reports indicated that the rebellion was widespread, perhaps even reaching all across the South, the governor had decided to send riders in all directions to alert and gather the militia. To play it safe, he had also ordered all units north and west of Richmond on alert. Then he had sent two Richmond units—one cavalry and one artillery—south toward Jerusalem. On top of all this, he had also dispatched a total of 2,000 guns and had ordered in the local militias of Norfolk, Portsmouth, and Petersburg.

Passions ran high all Tuesday afternoon as cavalry and artillery moved through the streets of Richmond. Rumors swept through the town, including one that a slave army was moving out of the Great Dismal Swamp and was heading toward the state capital.

By the Governor of the Commonwealth of Virginia,
A Proclamation.
Whereas the slave Nat, otherwise called Nat Turner, the contriver and leader of the late Insurrection in Southampton, is still going at large: Therefore I John Floyd, Governor of the Commonwealth of Virginia, have thought proper, and do hereby offer a reward of five hundred dollars to any person or persons who will apprehend and convey to the jail of Southampton County, the said slave Nat: And I do moreover require all officers civil and Military, and exhort the good people of the Commonwealth to use their best endeavors to cause the said fugitive to be apprehended, that he may be dealt with as the law directs. Given under my hand as Governor, and under the lesser seal of the Commonwealth at Richmond, this 17th day of September 1831.
John Floyd

Turner's revolt was quickly crushed by the white militia forces, but none of the slaveowners were prepared to rest as long as Turner remained at large. The governor of Virginia wrote this letter authorizing a reward of $500 for the capture of the rebel leader.

Mobs moved through the city, chasing and beating any blacks unfortunate enough to be seen on the street. "We experience much anxiety here," the governor said.

The seaport cities of Portsmouth and Norfolk were also seized by panic. Norfolk's mayor called in the U.S. Navy from Fort Monroe, convinced that the militia alone could not protect the city. Federal army and navy units were dispatched to Southampton County to back up the state militia.

In nearby Murfreesboro, North Carolina—just across the state line—one white man was so terrified by the news of a slave uprising that he fell dead of a heart attack on the street. All of the local militia were off at a revival meeting, and a rider was sent to alert them. He rode through the campsite, shouting, "The negroes have risen in Southampton and are

In the days immediately following the revolt, white lynch mobs carried out a wholesale slaughter of blacks in Southampton County. This crossroads was renamed Blackhead Signpost because the decapitated head of a slave was mounted on a pole by the side of the road.

killing every white person from the cradle up, and are coming this way!"

By Tuesday afternoon, the North Carolina Governor's Guards had assembled in Murfreesboro. By then, 3,000 armed whites were on the march toward Southampton County from neighboring counties in Virginia and North Carolina. This number included men from the U.S. Army and Navy, state and local militias, armed vigilante units, and lynch mobs.

The white reign of terror that soon began proved to be bloodier than the attacks by Turner and his men. Two detachments of cavalry from North Carolina killed 40 blacks in two days, decapitating 15 people and placing their heads on poles. At Cross Keys, five blacks were lynched by a mob. At a Barrow Road intersection, a man was beheaded and his skull was left to rot on a pole (called ever since "Blackhead Signpost"). Blacks were pulled from their cabins and were whipped, tortured, and lynched.

Over the next four days, more than 120 blacks were killed by lynch mobs and militia (a total that does not include the number of armed insurgents who had been captured and killed). The violence became so bad that the army commander, General Eppes, declared that any further atrocities would be dealt with under the Articles of War.

By Wednesday, August 31—10 days after the revolt had begun—49 rebels had been captured and imprisoned, including the badly wounded Hark Travis and Nelson Williams. Because slaves and free blacks were not entitled to a jury trial under Virginia law, a court trial known as "oyer and terminer" was held in Jerusalem to deal with the captured rebels. In such a hearing, the fate of each defendant is decided on by one or more judges rather than by a jury.

To give the trial an appearance of due process, lawyers were appointed for all of the slaves at a fee of $10 apiece. While the cases were being heard, the courthouse was surrounded by an angry, armed mob in the event that any of the defendants were acquitted. Every slave was priced as well as tried. Thus, when Hark was sentenced to death, the state had to pay the estate of his owner $450 for the pleasure of hanging him.

Court records and newspaper accounts show that anywhere from 15 to 20 men, and a few women, were hanged. Many more were sold back into slavery in areas with even more brutal conditions in the Caribbean and the Deep South.

The hangings went on for two weeks. Yet the panic continued in Virginia and spread west to the mountains, south into the Carolinas, and even north into Maryland and Delaware. For one question was on everyone's mind: Where was Nat Turner? ❧

9

THE FIRST
WAR

T HE "GREAT BANDITTI CHIEF," as the newspapers called Turner, was still at large long after all of his fellow rebels had been captured. The slaveowners did not rest easy. Posters and descriptions of him were sent out all over the state; he was described by Jerusalem lawyer William C. Parker (the same man who had led one of the patrols to find Turner and who was later appointed to "defend" him) as "between 30 and 35 years old—five feet six or 8 inches high—weighs between 150 & 160 rather bright complexion but not a mulatto—broad-shouldered—large flat nose—large eyes—broad flat feet rather knock kneed—walk brisk and active—hair on the top of the head very thin—no beard except on the upper lip and the top of the chin . . ."

The governor of Virginia put up a reward of $500, and this was added to by others until the price on Turner's head totaled $1,100. Ironically, he was worth far more as a rebel than the $400 he had brought as a slave.

By late September, posters of Turner were up all over North Carolina as well as Virginia. Rumors multiplied among both blacks and whites: "General Nat"

For two months following the end of the rebellion, Turner managed to evade the search parties that were hunting for him. He was finally captured on October 30, 1831, by Benjamin Phipps.

95

was hiding out in the mountains to the west; he had escaped to the Caribbean; he had been seen in the tall reeds near the Nottoway River "armed to the teeth." One story even had him spotted on an open road, walking with a Bible toward Ohio and the West, scattering seeds of rebellion much like Johnny Appleseed planted orchards across the country.

In fact, Turner was close by, hiding out in the woods and swamps that he knew so well. He had waited two days and two nights by Cabin Pond, hoping against hope that his men would return and his army would regroup. Then he had seen white men riding around, he later said, "as if looking for someone," and he concluded that his messengers had been captured and forced to betray his whereabouts. "On this," he wrote in his *Confessions*, "I gave up all hope for the present."

Turner then broke into the still-empty Travis house, which he knew well (the upstairs bedroom floors were still dark with the blood of his late owners) and found food, candles, and blankets. Then he literally went underground, hiding himself in a shallow cave that he dug under a pile of fence rails in an open field, figuring correctly that it was the last place that his pursuers would look. He spent sometime hiding out, perhaps contacting his wife (who had been savagely beaten but had never betrayed him) but more likely staying away to protect her and the children.

For a month, Turner ventured out solely at night, seeing only the still-secret supporters who must have provided him with food and water as well as news. His heart must have been heavy. He had seen Hark and Will shot down, and he surely must have been told that they had been captured and hanged and that Billy Artis had taken his own life rather than surrender.

However, Turner never gave up hope entirely. We know this because he never gave up his sword.

Even though it was useless as a weapon, it was the symbol of his rebellion and of his command, and he kept it by his side.

Turner's only hope for survival was to flee either to the West or to the sea, but individual survival had never been his goal. After all, he had escaped once and had come back for his people. So, in the end, he stayed with them, choosing to die in Southampton County rather than fleeing and living in exile.

As the days dragged on for Turner, and September turned into October, he pondered and brooded, praying for a sign that was never to come. He was almost caught on two separate occasions. One day, two slaves who were out hunting surprised him and betrayed

This cave was Turner's home for part of the time that he was in hiding.

him to their masters; he barely eluded the mob that subsequently came after him. Another time, Nathanial Francis spotted him and fired his weapon; the shot put a hole through Turner's hat. Once again he was pursued, so he dug another cave under a fallen sassafras deep in the woods. After spotting him for a second time, his pursuers knew for sure that he was in the neighborhood, and patrols with dogs began to comb the woods day and night.

On October 30, the inevitable happened. As Turner was crawling out of his carefully camouflaged tunnel, he was surprised by a white man holding a shotgun. The man, named Benjamin Phipps, ordered Turner to hand over his sword. He did, and his war against slavery was over.

Phipps tied up his captive and then fired into the air in triumph. (Ironically, Turner's captor was not a slaveowner but a poor white, of the kind whom Turner had ordered his men to spare.) Word of Turner's capture was soon out, and bells rang all across Southampton County as he was marched to a nearby plantation. Nearly a hundred people gathered around him, spitting in his face and taunting him.

Turner faced them back with a fierce pride, neither answering their taunts nor asking for mercy. A witness reported that he "just grinned" and refused to repent. At the nearby village of Cross Keys, he was beaten, then boarded up in a farmhouse for the night.

The infamous captive was carried in chains to Jerusalem on the following day. There he was taken before two judges—Trezevant and Parker—who began to question him. He answered them frankly and unrepentantly. His calm dignity amazed the reporters and observers who had crowded into the courtroom, expecting to see a crazed madman. He expressed no repentance over the deaths of the 55 to 60 whites who had been slain during the rebellion. He said only that had the rebellion been successful, "women and children would afterwards have been spared, and men too who ceased to resist."

The judges persisted. Hadn't he done wrong? they wanted to know. Didn't he feel remorse?

No, Turner insisted, he had done no wrong, even though the rebellion had failed. If he had to do it over, he said, he "must necessarily act in the same way again."

Turner's hearing was set for November 5, 1831. He was then carried to the jail, followed by an immense crowd reviling and cursing him. Inside the jail,

While Turner was in jail waiting for his trial to begin, two county judges questioned him about his revolt. The magistrates were startled to learn that Turner felt no remorse for his deeds and believed that he had been carrying out God's commandments.

THE

CONFESSIONS

OF

NAT TURNER,

LEADER OF THE LATE

Insurrection in Southampton, Va.

As fully and voluntarily made to Thos. C. Gray, in the prison where
he was confined—and acknowledged by him to be such, when
read before the court of Southampton, convened at
Jerusalem, November 5, 1831, for his trial.

*Shortly before his trial, Turner
had a meeting with a local lawyer
named Thomas Gray, during
which he discussed the reasons for
his revolt. Gray later published an
account of the conversation,
which he called* The Confessions
of Nat Turner.

MNEMOSYNE PUBLISHING INC.
Miami, Florida
1969

Barry Newsome and Thomas Haithcock, two free blacks who had ridden with him, were being held for hanging. While Turner was being chained and manacled, a white man taunted him, asking what had he done "with all the money he stole."

Turner replied coolly that he had taken exactly 75 cents. Then he turned to Newsome and Haithcock and said to them, "You know money was not my object."

Even in this grim setting, they laughed. Money? Freedom or death had been their object, and failing the one, they now were to have the other. Their motive was something that these slaveowners could not seem to understand.

On Tuesday, November 1, an elderly white man visited Turner's cell. He was Thomas Gray, a local lawyer, who had defended some of the insurgents. A friend of the jailer, he had received permission to transcribe Turner's story—his "confessions," as Gray called it—because public curiosity was "much on the stretch" to know the true story behind the rebellion.

For some reason—perhaps because Gray showed him a little decency and respect—Turner decided to talk to him. Although he told Gray the entire story, he omitted all of his rebels' names except for those whom he knew had been killed or hanged. Also, he never once mentioned his wife or his children. He explained most of his motives in religious terms, both because that was what he felt whites understood best and because he saw his devotion to freedom and liberty as a religious quest.

Indeed, when Gray asked Turner the same kind of question that the judges had asked him—Wasn't he sorry about what he had done, seeing that he was now to be punished with death?—he answered simply, "Was not Christ crucified?"

Gray ultimately attributed Turner's actions to revenge and religious fanaticism, and in several in-

NAT TURNER'S CONFESSION.

Agreeable to his own appointment, on the evening he was committed to prison, with permission of the jailer, I visited Nat on Tuesday, the first of November, when, without being questioned at all, he commenced his narrative in the following words:—

Sir,—You have asked me to give a history of the motives which induced me to undertake the late insurrection, as you call it. To do so, I must go back to the days of my infancy, and even before I was born. I was thirty-one years of age the 2d of October last, and born the property of Benj. Turner, of this county. In my childhood a circumstance occurred, which made an indelible impression on my mind, and laid the ground-work of that enthusiasm, which has terminated so fatally to many, both white and black, and for which I am about to atone on the gallows. It is here necessary to relate this circumstance—trifling as it may seem, it was the commencement of that belief which has grown with time, and even now, sir, in this dungeon, helpless and forsaken as I am, I cannot divest myself of it. Being at play with other children, when three or four years old, I was telling them something, which my mother overhearing, said it had happened before I was born—I stuck to my story, however, and related some things which went, in my opinion, to confirm it—others being called on were greatly astonished, knowing that these things had happened, caused them to say in my hearing, I surely would be a prophet, as the Lord had shewn me things that had happened before my birth. And my father and mother strengthened me in this my first impression, saying in my presence, I was intended for some great purpose, which they had always thought from certain marks on my head and breast—[a parcel of excrescences, which, I believe, are not at all uncommon, particularly among negroes, as I have seen several with the same. In this case, he had either cut them off, or they had nearly disappeared.] My grandmother, who was very religious, and to whom I was much attached—my master, who belonged to the church, and other religious persons who visited the house, and whom I often saw at prayers, noticing the singularity of my manners, I suppose, and my uncommon intelligence for a child, remarked I had too much sense to be raised, and if I was, I would never be of service to any one as a slave. To a mind like mine, restless, inquisitive, and observant of everything that was passing, it was easy to suppose that religion was the subject to which it would be directed, and, although this subject principally occupied my thoughts, there was nothing that I saw or heard of, to which my attention was not directed. The manner in which I learned to read and write, not only had great influence on my own mind, as I acquired it with the most perfect ease, so much so, that I have no recollection whatever of learning the alphabet, but, to the astonishment of the family, one day, when a book was shown me to keep me from crying, I began spelling the names of different objects—this was a source of wonder to all in the neighborhood, particularly the blacks—and this learning was constantly improved at all opportunities. When I got large enough to go to work, while employed, I was reflecting on many things that would present themselves to my imagination. and whenever an opportunity occurred of looking at a book, when the school-children were getting their lessons, I would find many things that the fertility of my own imagination had depicted to me before;

The Confessions *(whose first page is shown here) revealed Turner to be a man of high intelligence and moral purpose. Many people who read his statements were amazed to discover that he was not the crazed fanatic they imagined him to be.*

stances in the *Confessions*, he also put his own words in Turner's mouth. However, he seems to have recorded Turner's story pretty much as the revolt leader told it. All told, Gray was impressed by the dreaded rebel general. He said that he found Turner "for natural intelligence and quickness of apprehension, surpassed by few . . . he possesses an uncommon share of intelligence, with a mind capable of attaining anything."

Yet Gray was also horrified by what he said was Turner's "calm composure, still bearing the stains of the blood of helpless victims . . . covered with chains; yet daring to raise his manacled hands to Heaven, with a spirit soaring above the attributes of man. I looked upon him and my blood curdled in my veins." And rightly so. For what Gray was seeing was the very thing that "curdled the blood" of every slaveowner: their nightmare come to life—the slave who had seized back his own humanity with the sword.

It is not recorded that Turner had a last meeting in the jail with his wife and children. Perhaps such a meeting had already happened in secrecy, while he was still in hiding. After his capture, he seemed more careful than ever to protect them from the rage and terror that still gripped the whites of Southampton County and that had claimed so many lives of the innocent as well as of the "guilty" who had been his followers.

Turner's trial began on November 5. Such a huge crowd had gathered for it in Jerusalem that the sheriff had recruited extra deputies, fearing that the prisoner would be lynched on his way to the courthouse. The sheriff felt that it was important for Turner to be given the appearance of a fair trial.

After Turner was brought into the courtroom in chains, a clerk read the charges against him: "Nat, alias Nat Turner, a negro slave, the property of Putnam Moore, an infant, charged with conspiring to rebel and making insurrection."

William Parker, who was appointed as Turner's defense attorney, acted fairly, and on the instructions of his client (and probably to his own surprise), he entered a plea of not guilty. Turner informed his lawyer, the courtroom, and the judge very clearly that he felt no guilt whatsoever.

The first person to testify against Turner was a man named Waller who had managed to escape from one of the farms that was ravaged by the rebels. He stated that Turner did in fact command the rebels who had killed his wife and children. Turner did not dispute this.

Next, Judge Trezevant took the stand and repeated the testimony that Turner had given to him on the day after his capture. The clerk then read the long statement that Turner had given to Gray (later published as the *Confessions*), which Turner acknowledged to be "full, free and voluntary."

Turner received a quick trial at the Southampton County Courthouse. He made no effort to deny that he had committed the deeds of which he was accused, stating that only God could pass judgment on him.

That was it for the trial. Turner was quickly pronounced guilty, and he was asked by Judge Cobb, "Have you anything to say why sentence of death should not be pronounced upon you?"

"Nothing but what I've said before," Turner replied calmly.

The judge then delivered a long and passionate speech on the horrors of rebellion. His voice rose in pitch as he concluded, "The judgment of this court is that you . . . on Friday next, between the hours of 10 A.M. and 2 P.M. be hung by the neck until you are dead! dead! dead! and may the Lord have mercy upon your soul." Turner was then valued at $375, which the judge ordered to be paid to the Moore estate.

On the appointed day—November 11, 1831—Turner went unflinchingly to the death that he had chosen over slavery. He was not the first—nor would he be the last—black rebel to be hanged in the aftermath of the rebellion. In all, 50 stood trial and 21 were hanged. There were at least 20—and perhaps

Shortly after Turner's rebellion, one anguished American commented, "I foresee that this land must one day or another, become a field of blood." The sacrifices made by Turner's revolutionaries and countless numbers of other antislavery fighters helped bring on the Civil War and a new era of freedom for all black Americans.

as many as 30—more rebellion-related "legal" executions (not including outright lynchings) in neighboring Virginia counties and in North Carolina. Whether these were actually related to Turner's rebellion, or only thought to be so by the panicked whites, is not known. All told, the rebellion cost the lives of approximately 60 whites and as many as 200 blacks.

But the heavy toll of slavery and rebellion did not stop there. After all, slaves were property; and whereas hangings brought personal satisfaction to many whites, destroying property brought financial hardship. Consequently, the governor commuted the sentences of 10 convicted slaves who were then sold south. Among them were Turner's wife and daughter.

According to folklore, one of Turner's sons found his way to relative freedom in Ohio. Another is said to have stayed in Southampton County. Even today, near the town of Jerusalem (now called Courtland) there is a black storekeeper named Turner who proudly claims to be Nat Turner's direct descendant.

And well might this man be proud. For although Nat Turner's rebellion did not end in triumph, neither did it result in failure. By mobilizing and leading a slave army, he destroyed forever the notion that the slaves would not, or could not, fight for their freedom. In seeking racial justice and human rights, he became the spiritual father and political inspiration to subsequent generations of freedom fighters, from antislavery activist Harriet Tubman to the 200,000 black soldiers who took up arms against southern slaveowners during the Civil War, to such 20th-century black activists as Marcus Garvey and Malcolm X.

In black folklore, "The Second War" is a phrase that is often used to refer to the Civil War, a bloody struggle that put an end to slavery in America. "The First War" was the rebellion led by Nat Turner.

Nat Turner's Death Certificate

CHRONOLOGY

—◖◗—

1800	Nat Turner is born in Southampton County, Virginia
1821	Runs away from Samuel Turner's estate; marries Cherry
1822	Is sold to Thomas Moore and is forced to live apart from his family
1825	Becomes a preacher
1828	Begins to recruit men for a slave rebellion
Aug. 22, 1831	The slave rebellion begins
Oct. 30, 1831	Turner is captured
Nov. 1, 1831	Has his "confessions" recorded by Thomas Gray
Nov. 5, 1831	Is put on trial
Nov. 11, 1831	Is hanged in Jerusalem, Virginia

FURTHER READING

Aptheker, Herbert. *Afro-American History: The Modern Era.* New York: Citadel Press, 1971.

———. *Nat Turner's Slave Rebellion.* New York: Humanities Press, 1966.

Bennett, Lerone, Jr. *Before the Mayflower.* New York: Penguin, 1984.

Clarke, John Henrik, ed. *William Styron's Nat Turner: Ten Black Writers Respond.* Boston: Greenwood, 1968.

Drewry, William Sydney. *The Southampton Insurrection.* Washington, D.C.: Johnson, 1900.

Harding, Vincent. *There Is a River.* New York: Harcourt Brace Jovanovich, 1981.

Oates, Stephen B. *The Fires of Jubilee: Nat Turner's Fierce Rebellion.* New York: New American Library, 1975.

Rogers, J. A. *World's Great Men of Color.* New York: Macmillan, 1972.

Rollins, Charlemae Hill. *They Showed the Way.* New York: Thomas Y. Crowell, 1964.

Tragle, Henry Irving, ed. *The Southampton Slave Revolt of Eighteen Thirty-One.* Amherst: University of Massachusetts Press, 1971.

INDEX

110

PICTURE CREDITS

TERRY BISSON is a graduate of the University of Louisville in Kentucky. He is the author of two novels, *Wyrldmaker* and *Talking Man*. He has also written articles on history and political affairs for *The Nation* and the *City Sun*. His third novel, entitled *Fire on the Mountain* and based on events in the life of John Brown, will be published by Arbor House in 1988. He lives in New York City with his wife and children.

NATHAN IRVIN HUGGINS is W.E.B. Du Bois Professor of History and Director of the W.E.B. Du Bois Institute for Afro-American Research at Harvard University. He previously taught at Columbia University. Professor Huggins is the author of numerous books, including *Black Odyssey: The Afro-American Ordeal in Slavery*, *The Harlem Renaissance*, and *Slave and Citizen: The Life of Frederick Douglas*.